FROM STRESS
TO WELL-BEING

**CONTEMPORARY CHRISTIAN
COUNSELING**

FROM STRESS TO WELL-BEING

CRAIG W. ELLISON, PH.D.

CONTEMPORARY CHRISTIAN COUNSELING

General Editor
GARY R. COLLINS, PH.D.

Library of Congress Cataloging-in-Publication Data:

Ellison, Craig W., 1944–
    From Stress to Well-Being/Craig W. Ellison
    p. cm.—(Contemporary Christian Counseling)
    Includes bibliographical references and index.
    ISBN 0–8499–0875–2:
    1. Pastoral counseling. 2. Pastoral psychology. 3. Stress (Psy-
chology)—Religious aspects—Christianity. I. Title. II. Series.
BV4012.2.E45   1994
253.5'2—dc20   93–1699
                                            CIP

3 4 5 6 7 8 9 LBM 7 6 5 4 3 2 1

Printed in the United States of America

Contents

Preface

For many years I have been concerned about the interface of biblical perspectives and contemporary psychology. In previous books, such as *Saying Goodbye to Loneliness and Finding Intimacy*; *Your Better Self: Christianity, Psychology and Self-Esteem*; and *Healing for the City: Counseling in the Urban Setting*, I have attempted to interface the two with regard to limited topic areas. I have been concerned for some time, however, that most of the integrative thinking that has been done in evangelical Christian psychological circles has not been very heuristic. Since at least the mid-1980s little has happened in terms of integrative advance. What theories we do have appear to be static and lack the dynamism that ought to be present in an integrative approach describing the complexity and vibrancy of human beings.

The psychospiritual counseling approach presented in *From Stress to Well-Being* represents an interaction of biblical investigation, contemporary personality theories, and clinical experience. As I have formulated this approach over the past seven to ten years, I have seen its effectiveness as I have used it either implicitly or explicitly with hundreds of clients. I have also benefited from the feedback of dozens of seminary students in classes at the Alliance Theological Seminary.

The roots of psychospiritual counseling are in my study of the Scriptures, but my study of psychology over the past thirty years has clearly been formative as well. Psychospiritual counseling is not a totally unique approach, but it is more complete than any existing secular or Christian approaches that I am aware of. As such, I believe that it more completely pictures the complex, systemic nature of human beings. A number of other Christian and secular approaches have looked at one or two of the psychospiritual needs of people, but none have considered as many as eight interactive needs. Psychospiritual counseling focuses primarily upon human beings as spiritual, psychological, and social beings. It recognizes the importance of biological factors in the creation and responses to stress as well.

The psychospiritual counseling model represented in figure 1.1 is developmental. It begins at the beginning . . . at the point of God's creation of Adam and Eve in his image. Chapter 2 presents the biblical foundation of this approach, describing the ontological givens (the givens of being) woven into human personality by God, and the distress that resulted from the Fall. Instead of unbroken *shalom* (well-being), post-Fall humanity has experienced considerable *stress* (distress, pain). Human beings find themselves trying to return to the pre-Fall experience of well-being. Depending upon the avenues chosen, however, attempts to avoid and remove pain may create even greater distress as various psychospiritual deficits or needs are not met in ways that God intended.

The story of how human development frequently leads to experiences of distress and to the creation of psychological structures that promote lifelong stress is found in chapters 2–7. Biological, interpersonal, cognitive, perceptual, and personality factors are frequently shaped and distorted in ways that increase the long-range buildup of distress and ultimate disintegration of a person. Chapters 7 and 8 examine the crucial place of choice in the experience of stress and *shalom*, showing how a person may either proceed down a path toward greater distress and destruction or may choose an immediately difficult but ultimately healthy Upward Path that brings well-being. Chapters 9–12 examine some of the basic principles of psychospiritual counseling and focus on emotional, interpersonal, and spiritual counseling interventions.

From Stress to Well-Being is filled with case illustrations. It is important to note that in all cases names and identifying information has been removed. Although all of the illustrations come from my counseling experience, many of them are composites of several clients with similar problems.

It is my hope that this book will stimulate a significant step ahead in integrative thinking about the interface of biblical understanding and psychological knowledge. I hope that *From Stress to Well-Being* will be built upon and improved; it is certainly not the last word. I find that as time goes on I continue to see additional implications and connections. The book, in that sense, is incomplete. It is also my hope that the model and ideas given will stimulate research. To that end, I have been working on the development of the Psychospiritual Needs Inventory, which is based on the concepts of ontological givens/psychospiritual needs and has potential for helpful clinical use in years ahead. In addition, I hope that others will find the material presented here practically helpful in their Christian counseling. I have used these concepts to guide my counseling, and at times, have presented the structure given in figure 1.1 directly to clients. In both cases, I feel that counselees have been helped.

Finally, I want to express special appreciation for the indefatigable Gary Collins, without whose faith, encouragement, and continuing enthusiasm this book would have never reached birth. Also, thanks to Terri Gibbs and the folks at Word who patiently waited for me to complete this project in the midst of multiple demands on my time and energy. I genuinely appreciated Lois Stück, whose sensitive and thorough copyediting was a tremendous help. I am grateful to the Alliance Theological Seminary for providing a sabbatical, which helped me to do much of the initial draft of this book, and especially to Helen Ellenberger for her cheerful and competent assistance. My wife, Sharon, has travailed with me in the birth of yet another book, and I am deeply thankful for her perseverance.

Chapter One

The Nature of Stress: An Overview

THE EFFECTS OF STRESS UPON HUMAN HEALTH and well-being are staggering. At least $60 billion is lost every year due to stress-related physical illnesses.[1] Heart disease, which is associated with stress, results in an annual loss of more than 135 million workdays in the United States. Approximately 75–85 percent of all industrial accidents are caused by the inability to cope with stress. These accidents have cost United States companies more than $32 billion in a given year.[2] Over 230 million prescriptions are written annually to relieve feelings of stress and anxiety in the United States. At least 25 million Americans suffer from high blood pressure, more than 8 million have stomach ulcers, and over 12 million people turn to alcohol in response to our stress-filled age.[3]

Migraine headaches, chronic fatigue, bruxism (gnashing of teeth), kidney disorders, hardening of the arteries, heart disease, gastric or duodenal ulcers, anorexia nervosa, motor disturbances, and stuttering are often connected with prolonged and excessive stress.[4] Other signs of stress include muscle twitching or tightness, insomnia, shortness of breath, asthma, heart fluttering, and substantial weight gain or loss.

Stress also affects the ways that we think and feel. Stress is associated with adjustment disorders, conduct disorders (hostility/aggression), neuroses, psychoses,[5] addictive behaviors,[6] and anxiety. Chronically and extremely stressed people do not think as well. They are more likely to distort situations, be indecisive, and have unproductive and ruminative patterns of thinking. Memory and concentration may also be impaired.[7]

A stressed person normally displays either a fight or flight pattern of behavior. The fight response may be shown in physical aggression, irritability, argumentativeness, or a tendency to overreact to relatively minor situations. A flight response involves trying to avoid or leave the situation physically, or through fantasy, emotional detachment, or passivity.[8]

Stress is also associated with frequent mood swings, feelings of being overwhelmed, depression, loss of motivation, preoccupation or absent-mindedness, and spiritual flatness. While none of these symptoms by themselves may be due to stress, a combination of them makes it very likely that a person is under significant stress.

Les was under tremendous pressure. As a real estate broker, the housing recession had left him without a sales commission for five months. He had run out of ideas to generate buyers. Les and his wife Barbara estimated that they had only two months of their personal savings left. Although they had never had a great marriage, now they constantly argued with each other. Things were so bad that they slept in different rooms. Les had no idea how he would be able to provide for his four children after their savings were depleted. The youngest child had a heart abnormality and still needed at least one more major surgery. Les' parents had not spoken to him for over two years, since he had taken Barbara's side in a family dispute. He felt that there was no one he could talk with who would really understand him. Recently, he was unable to sleep for more than three hours at a time. He had also begun drinking heavily again, after abstaining for almost two years. He tried to see a counselor but felt that it did little good. It seemed there was no solution. Unless. . . . On an early Thursday morning in November, police scuba divers pulled the body of a five-foot ten-inch man in his late thirties out of the river.

BACKGROUND

Hans Selye, the father of modern stress theory and research, defined stress as "the nonspecific response of the body to any demand."[9] Based on several decades of medical research that focused primarily on the physiology of stress, Selye and others concluded that stressors increase the demand on a person for readjustment and adaptation. In response to stress the body tries to reestablish a state of prior physiological balance or normalcy. Selye identified the existence of a three-stage General Adaptation Syndrome (GAS), which describes the physically destructive impact of exposure to prolonged or extreme stressors.[10] Selye found that severe and chronic stress can result in organ damage and possible death due to the wear and tear placed upon the body by the adaptation process.

Subsequent research has confirmed that excessive stress is linked with poor physical health because of the demands made on the body. Stressors activate the hypothalamus portion of the brain, which stimulates the autonomic nervous system. As a result, the heart speeds up, the digestive tract slows down, and the pituitary gland is stimulated. The person is being prepared physically to meet the threat (stressor) with a fight or flight response. The posterior lobe of the pituitary releases vasopressin, which constricts arterial walls and increases blood pressure. The anterior lobe of the pituitary gland releases hormones ACTH and TSH, which stimulate the thyroid gland to increase metabolism. ACTH prompts the adrenal cortex, in turn, to release anti-inflammatory glucocorticoids, which then stimulate the pancreas to increase the level of blood sugar.

While all this is happening, the autonomic nervous system triggers the adrenal medulla to release adrenaline and noradrenaline. These hormones stimulate the cardiovascular system. The result of this autonomic hormonal activity is an

increase in heart rate, blood supply to the muscles, blood
pressure, metabolism of oxygen, and breathing rate. The stress-
activated endocrine response persists and has a wear-and-tear
effect on the body.[11]

Selye distinguished between two types of stress. *Eustress* is the
stimulation needed to lift our lives from boredom and motivate
us to interact with our environments. It is not unpleasant or debilitating. *Distress*, on the other hand, is unpleasant and eventually
produces deterioration, disintegration, and disease. In this book,
stress is used as a shortened form of the word *distress* or *emotional pain*.

The goal is to find ways to minimize and manage stress that
are consistent with God's guidelines for healthy living and to
promote the experience of well-being. In Selye's terms, this is
done by minimizing distress and facilitating eustress.[12]

CURRENT PERSPECTIVES

More often than not the stressors that people face are
psychosocial. A brochure advertising the Third International
Montreux Congress on Stress stated that "the nature of contemporary stress is more apt to be mental than physical.
Unfortunately, our bodies still automatically respond in the
same stereotyped fashion. . . ."

The autonomic and endocrine reactions occur in response to
any stressor. It does not matter whether the stressor is physical, psychosocial, or spiritual. *Whenever a person is confronted by
anything that is perceived as threatening or challenging, the body
responds by preparing for fight or flight.* This, of course, is why an
interpersonally bad day at the office may leave us with tight
muscles, irritability, and excess energy. Often people seem to
come home from such a day just spoiling for a fight. The bad
day has triggered general alarm syndrome responses in our
bodies, but we have not been able to release the energy (unless
we were smart enough to vigorously exercise after work). We
are not permitted to punch a coworker in the nose or to run
away from the office in the face of stress. If these stresses continue and are not properly managed, we get hypertension,
colitis, ulcers, migraine headaches, or muscle spasms, or we
displace our fight/flight responses onto our families.

Surprisingly, no universally accepted definition of stress has been propounded by stress researchers. Most agree, however, that stress is a response to some kind of information that is interpreted as a threat. Past experience and the patterns of individual personality serve as interpretive grids that guide whether or not we respond to a stimulus as a possible danger to health and well-being. It is most helpful for the counselor to view stress as "a relationship between the person and the environment that is appraised as taxing or exceeding his or her resources and endangering his or her well-being."[13] Stress is triggered whenever well-being is threatened. It is often experienced physically as tension and emotionally as anxiety, depression, pain, or feeling overwhelmed.

The sources of threat (stressors) may be objective or subjective dangers. Researchers have tried to classify stressors according to

duration—whether the stressor is acute and time-limited, chronic and intermittent, or chronic and continuous;[14]

quality of the stressor event—major changes affecting large numbers of people, major changes affecting one or a few, or daily hassles;

quantity of stressors—life-change units.

Without individual perception being considered, however, the research to date seems to have relatively little clinical value.[15]

Although considerable effort has been made to find objective ways to measure various stressors,[16] particularly through the investigation of life events or life changes,[17] the importance of the individual's perception in determining the experience of stress is significant. *Perception* is the meaning that a specific person associates with a particular stimulus. It is based on the *stimulus event* (what is actually happening), *previous stress experiences* that the person has had with similar stimuli, and *developmental history*. (Developmental history includes what a person has learned to regard as threatening and how the person has learned to cope with stress.) These patterns of perception and response make up much of what we call personality. Anyone who has counseled for a period of time has experienced the importance of personal patterns. For example, some people who are confronted by the highly stressful events of death or divorce disintegrate and become incapacitated. Others are strongly impacted but come to grips with their trauma and remain well-integrated, healthy people.

Even in situations of traumatic stress where everyone is affected by the same stressor, there are individual variations in both the appraisal and response. Even if more finely tuned measures of objective stressors are developed, counselors will still need to gauge the subjective evaluations that counselees make. Roskies has correctly pointed out:

> Many elements contribute to the individual's stress appraisal (e.g., perception of external environment, perception of coping resources, pattern of commitments, values and beliefs that increase or decrease vulnerability to specific types of threats or challenges, etc.); therefore, we can expect not only that individuals will vary in their appraisal of stressors, but also that the same individual will make quite different appraisals of the same stress trigger at different times or in different contexts.[18]

AN INTEGRATIVE FRAMEWORK

Figure 1.1 presents a simplified developmental framework for understanding the nature of stress and the goal of Christian counseling. Each chapter of this book focuses on a portion of the model. This framework is designed to help the counselor systematically analyze the nature of stress from an integrative, psychospiritual perspective. The goal of psychospiritual counseling is to aid the counselee's movement toward *shalom* (well-being) and away from greater stress, pain, and disintegration.

Psychospiritual counseling begins with a biblical overview of human nature and need. Adam and Eve originally lived in a state of complete *shalom* (wholeness, contentment, joy, peace, and integrity), experiencing the well-being of having been

A Psychospiritual Model of Christian Counseling

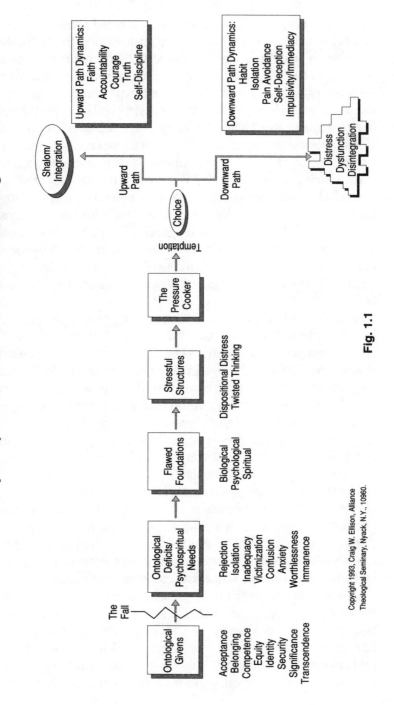

Fig. 1.1

Copyright 1993, Craig W. Ellison, Alliance
Theological Seminary, Nyack, N.Y., 10960.

made in God's image. *Shalom* was shattered when Satan successfully seduced them into trying to shrug off the limitations
of their creatureliness and to exercise their freedom of choice
as though they were divinely sovereign, without boundaries
or accountability. Immediately, their experience of *shalom* became an experience of shame and stress. Their very beings
were structurally twisted. Brokenness replaced wholeness,
defensiveness replaced delight, distress replaced *shalom*. From
the moment of the Fall, no human being (except the incar-
nate Christ) has ever fully recovered the *shalom* that God
intended for mankind on this side of eternity. And yet we all
long to recover Eden. We struggle and look for ways to escape
the effects of the original ontological twisting that leaves us as
the carriers of the sin condition. Indeed, as the Psalmist de-
clared, we are conceived in sin (see Ps. 51:5), experiencing the
pain and stress of disorder and brokenness from the beginning
of life.

The first three chapters of Genesis suggest eight givens of
being made in the image of God (ontological givens) and the
psychospiritual distress that is basic to the human experience
due to the deficits of those givens because of original sin. As
they attempt to avoid psychospiritual distress and experience
well-being, people often develop faulty patterns of coping that
ultimately lead to greater stress. Psychospiritual counseling
helps people to identify destructive, stress-intensifying patterns and replace them through healthy choices that lead to
consistent experiences of *shalom*.

Certain biological, psychosocial, and spiritual factors encountered during childhood and adolescence have a stress-
generating impact upon a child's orientation toward life. Some
of them fill a child with overwhelming pain that is carried into
adulthood as residual stress; others create flawed foundations
of perception and response that create and intensify stress.

People acquire a variety of stressful personality and thought
structures during childhood. These structures are intended to
help the person deal with the pain of psychospiritual distress.
Unfortunately, many of the patterns are ultimately destructive
and do not lead to consistent *shalom*. Personality, ego defense
patterns, self-perception, gender, faulty filters, and rotten rules

may generate and amplify stress by affecting the ways in which life is perceived and responded to.

Several types of potential stressors, either by themselves or through interaction with a person's residual stress and faulty coping patterns, result in a buildup of stress. This "pressure cooker" includes biological, environmental, institutional, psychosocial, and spiritual sources of contemporary stress.

It is when a person is under significant stress due to both current stressors and residual stress that temptation is usually strongest. Temptation is essentially an invitation to choose in ways that give immediate relief from stress but that later result in magnified stress, dysfunction, and disintegration. This might be considered a Downward Path. If a person resists temptation and chooses the Upward Path, however, the end result will be increased levels of *shalom*, or physical, interpersonal, emotional, and spiritual well-being. Choices that are made out of habit, isolation, a primary pain avoidance concern, deception, and impulsivenss or immediacy lead to the Downward Path consequences of even greater distress, dysfunction, and disintegration. The Downward Path is the path to ultimate pain and destruction.

Upward Path choices inevitably involve some degree of pain due to the need to say *no* to Downward Path options that are attractive and promise immediate pain relief but produce long-term deterioration. Upward Path choices are grounded in faith, accountability, courage, truth, and self-discipline. The consequence of consistent Upward Path living is *shalom*, as expressed in emotional maturity, healthy relationships, physical health, and spiritual well-being.

Psychospiritual counseling is based on an open universe understanding of the nature of human problems and of potential counseling interventions. This approach allows for a constructive integration of natural (science) and special revelation (the Bible) sources of knowledge about human need and healing. It begins with the psychospiritual preparation of the counselor as a born-again believer who is in active communion with God through his Word and the activity of the Holy Spirit in the counselor's life. As a result of this relationship, the counselor is able to be a channel of God's wisdom, grace, power, and healing. As a professionally trained counselor, he or she is further able to apply specific intervention possibilities to encourage healing of emotions, relationships, self, and the spirit.

NOTES

1. U. S. Clearinghouse for Mental Health Information, 1982. Reported in Michael. T. Matteson and John. M. Ivancevich, *Controlling Work Stress: Effective Human Resource and Management Strategies* (San Francisco: Jossey-Bass, 1987).

2. National Safety Council, College of Insurance and National Institute for Occupational Safety and Health, 1984. Reported in Matteson and Ivancevich, *Controlling Work Stress.*

3. Keith W. Sehnert, *Stress/Unstress: How You Can Control Stress at Home and on the Job* (Minneapolis: Augsburg, 1981), 14.

4. Hans Selye, "The Stress Concept Today," in *Handbook on Stress and Anxiety,* ed. Irwin L. Kutash, Louis B. Schlesinger and Associates (San Francisco: Jossey-Bass, 1980), 127–43.

5. Joseph D. Noshpitz and R. Dean Coddington, eds., *Stress and the Adjustment Disorders* (New York: Wiley, 1990).

6. Patricia Wuertzer and Lucinda May, *Relax, Recover: Stress Management for Recovering People* (Minneapolis: Hazelden, 1988).

7. American Psychiatric Association, *Diagnostic and Statistical Manual of Mental Disorders,* 3d rev. ed. (Washington, D.C.: American Psychiatric Association, 1987).

8. Dorothy H. G. Cotton, *Stress Management: An Integrated Approach to Therapy* (New York: Brunner-Mazel, 1990).

9. Hans Selye, *Stress without Distress* (New York: Lippincott, 1974), 14.

10. Hans Selye, *The Stress of Life* (New York: McGraw-Hil, 1956).

11. D. Adams, *Understanding and Managing Stress* (San Diego: University Associates, 1980).

12. Selye, "Stress Concept," 141.

13. R. S. Lazarus and S. Folkman, *Stress, Appraisal and Coping* (New York: Springer, 1984), 21.

14. G. R. Elliott and C. Eisdorfer, *Stress and Human Health* (New York: Springer, 1982).

15. Ethel Roskies, *Stress Management for the Healthy Type A: Theory and Practice* (New York: Guilford, 1987).

16. Andrew E. Skodol et al., "The Nature of Stress: Problems of Measurement," in *Stressors and the Adjustment Disorders,* ed. Joseph D. Noshpitz and R. Dean Coddington (New York: Wiley, 1990), 3–20.

17. Thomas H. Holmes and R. H. Rahe, "The Social Readjustment Rating Scale," *Journal of Psychosomatic Research* 11 (1967): 213–18.

18. Roskies, *Stress Management,* 35.

Chapter Two

In the Beginning . . .

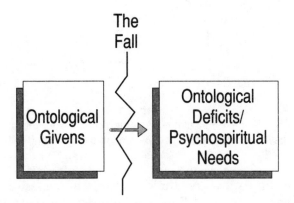

IN THE BEGINNING, THERE WAS NO STRESS. Once creation was complete, everything existed as God intended. All of the parts fit together perfectly in a state of total spiritual, psychological, and relational harmony (see figure 2.1). Adam and Eve were the prototypes of all that human beings were meant to be. Made in God's image, they were whole, unified beings who functioned as well-balanced, integrated systems.[1]

They were relational beings who fully enjoyed harmonious relationships with God and with each other. Completely reflecting God's character, they enjoyed the highest level of *shalom*, or well-being. In almost two-thirds of its 250 appearances in Scripture, the term *shalom* refers to a state of fulfillment that results from God's presence and covenantal relationship.[2] Its root meaning includes the concepts of completeness, wholeness, and harmony or well-being.[3] *Shalom* is the positive life experience of a person who is functioning the way that God intended.

Human Beings as God Intended

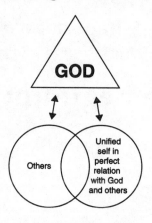

Fig. 2.1.
The Pre-Fall state of spiritual, interpersonal, and
psychological harmony experienced by Adam and Eve.

According to the first three chapters in Genesis, the well-being that Adam and Eve experienced stemmed from the fact that they perfectly reflected God's image. As unbroken reflections of their creator, they related to God, to each other, and to themselves without distortion and defensiveness. Their experience was one of complete acceptance, belonging, competence, equity, identity, security, significance, and transcendence.

Figure 2.2 indicates some of the biblical foundation in Genesis for identifying these ontological givens (fundamental characteristics of their being that were rooted in their wholeness and completeness). There are many other direct and indirect references to these qualities throughout the Bible.

ONTOLOGICAL GIVENS

Ontological givens are psychospiritual qualities that reflect the image and creative work of God. They are interactive and not totally independent from each other. For example, it is probably not possible to completely separate experiences of

Ontological Givens in Early Genesis

Acceptance	Gen. 1:31a; 2:25; 3:8 (implied)
Belonging	Gen. 2:18, 20, 21–24
Competence	Gen. 1:28; 2:15, 19–20
Equity	Gen. 2:16–17; 3:1
Identity	Gen. 1:26–27; 2:24; 3:20
Security	Gen. 1:28–30; 2:8–9
Significance	Gen. 1:26, 31
Transcendence	Gen. 1:27; 2:7; 3:4–5, 8–24

Fig. 2.2

acceptance and belonging from each other. Ontological givens describe the psychological, interpersonal, and spiritual characteristics of fully functioning human beings. Taken together, the presence of these qualities may be viewed as healthy personality or the fully rational True Self that God intended for human beings when he created them in his image.

The ontological given of *acceptance* refers to an inner sense of being okay, without condemnation, guilt, or shame about who one is. Acceptance reflects the "very good" evaluation of God as he assessed his creation (see Gen. 1:31). Acceptance is the result of self-evaluation based on internalized standards of goodness as well as on feedback received from people who are emotionally important to us.

Belonging has to do with feelings of being united with another person or persons; a sense of desired intimacy, closeness, and attachment to one or more others. It is giving and receiving love. To belong is to feel part of a relationship, organization, or movement that is bigger than one's individual self. The interpersonal essence of human beings as reflective of God's character is certainly implied in Genesis 1:26 and 2:18. Adam's need for intimacy is clearly implied in God's evaluation that it was not good for Adam to be alone, and in God's provision of a woman who was "bone of [his] bones and flesh of [his] flesh" to whom man is to cleave (Gen. 2:23–24).

Competence is the ability to choose and conduct one's self so as to experience the positive rewards/consequences with regard to one's choices and conduct. It involves a sense of adequacy and success. It is believing that one's life is significantly under one's own control. It is seeing one's self as being able to manage one's life constructively. God regarded Adam and Eve as competent by virtue of his assignment for them to rule over (see Gen. 1:28) and manage (see Gen. 2:15) the created order.

Equity is an internal sense of rightness, wrongness, and fairness. It is an innate human moral orientation (Rom. 1:19–20; 2:14–15). Prior to the Fall, human morality perfectly reflected the holiness and righteousness of God. Satan, in fact, appealed to Eve's sense of equity by questioning the limitations that God had placed upon Adam and Eve as unfair and, in effect, calling God a liar (see Gen. 3:1–5). After the Fall, human beings have retained a sense of moral "oughtness" in every society. The human need for rules and some system of ethical order reflects this given, even though it is often distorted by finitude and egocentricity and untempered by mercy. When standards of rightness and fairness are violated, there is usually some sense of moral outrage, and those suffering from the violations feel victimized and diminished.

Identity is a self-discerned pattern of characteristic choices and behaviors that are relatively consistent for a person over time and across situations. Identity is the capacity to recognize one's self as being both separate from and more than an extension of others. Identity is partially shaped by the descriptions that emotionally significant others make of us, the values that we embrace, and our own observations of our patterns and preferences. Out of our identity comes the initiative to proactively accomplish self-selected goals and purposes. Adam and Eve had a clear sense of identity as man and woman (see Gen. 2:23), as husband and wife (see Gen. 2:24), as specially created beings made in God's image and breathed into with the breath of life (see Gen. 2:7), and as ruler and manager (see Gen. 2:19–20).

Security is the experience of feeling safe. It is feeling physically, emotionally, and spiritually protected. It is *not* feeling helpless, vulnerable, or exposed. It is feeling cared for and out of danger. Adam and Eve were secure (see Gen. 2:25) until they rejected the boundaries God had put around them to protect them from disaster (see Gen. 3:8–10). Satan painted those moral/spiritual boundary lines as unfair and restrictive—demeaning to those who ought to see themselves as sovereign gods living in absolute freedom. The moment that Adam and Eve sinned (ignored the boundaries), they felt vulnerable, exposed, and anxious.

Significance is the emotional belief that I matter, that I am somebody of value (compared to a void or nothing). It is the feeling that I count, that I am important and worthwhile. This is conveyed in Genesis through the special creation of Adam and Eve, by their placement at the apex of the created order, by the responsibility given to them, by the fact that God regularly spent time with them, and by the attention that Satan paid to them.

Transcendence refers to a sense of meaning and purpose for life that stems from one's relationship with God. It is the ability to discover and experience patterns of life-meaning that go beyond the purely natural. It is being connected with God and eternal purposes. It is expressed in a sense of dynamic psychospiritual connection with God and orderedness that goes beyond the immediate physical senses.

It is important to note that these ontological qualities reflect the psychospiritual unity of human nature as created and intended by God. Although all of the qualities that we have suggested as ontological givens have been discussed by secular psychologists from a strictly *psychological* perspective, our contention is that they are *not* purely psychological qualities. Rather, they are *psychospiritual* qualities that reflect the fundamental integration of human nature as soul and spirit. Scripture throughout recognizes the wholeness of human personality and the difficulty of distinguishing between soul and spirit (see Heb. 4:12).

THE UNIFIED PERSON

Beginning with the Old Testament, human beings are regarded as whole persons. They are not viewed as distinctly separable parts that operate semi-independently. While various terms are used (*nephesh, basar, ruach*), these words are partially interchangeable and point to the unity of the person. The Hebrews even viewed the soul as almost physical and the physical parts of humans as having psychical functions, so that all behavior represented the whole person.[4]

The New Testament use of the term *soul* also refers to the whole person, existing in bodily form, and is no different from the holistic thought of the Old Testament.[5] Both the Old Testament and New Testament words for *flesh* (*basar, sarx*), *soul* (*nephesh, psyche*) and *spirit* (*ruach, pneuma*), refer to the whole person, although each has partially distinctive meanings.

J. K. Howard argues:

> In terms of biblical psychology, man does not have a "soul," he is one. He is a living and vital whole. It is possible to distinguish between his activities but we cannot distinguish between the parts, for they have no independent existence. Man is an entity, quite indivisible into his various elements, even though aspects of his personality, such as appetites, his affections, his moral purposes, may be examined and handled one by one, just as we can look at each side of a coin in turn.[6]

Certainly the concept of organismic unity is implied in the theology of the resurrection body (see 1 Cor. 15) and in such passages as 1 Thessalonians 5:23, "May your whole spirit, soul and body be kept blameless at the coming of our Lord Jesus Christ." The weight of Scripture is clearly in the direction of viewing persons as systems.

We are unified, interactive, and interdependent beings. We are composed of identifiable but not independent subsystems (i.e., body, soul, spirit). Each subsystem of our being influences and is influenced by the other. How we feel physically (body) affects how we think, feel, relate to others and make choices (soul) and the quality of our spiritual well-being (spirit). Our psychological state (soul) impacts our spiritual and physical well-being. Finally, our spiritual state may influence our soul and body functioning.[7] Figure 2.3 illustrates this view of human beings as systemic in nature. The *body* refers to our

Human Beings Are Integrated Systems

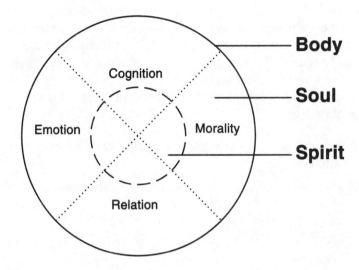

Fig. 2.3. Each system (body, soul, spirit) and
subsystem is interconnected to make a unified self.

physical state; *soul* refers to how we think, feel, relate and
choose; *spirit* refers to the synthesizing core of our being that
interacts with our soul to produce moral choice and behavior.

In the pre-Fall character of Adam and Eve, perfection or
maturity (*teleos* in the New Testament) was expressed in their
unbroken wholeness. Wholeness in the Old Testament is con-
ceptually related to the notions of holiness and healthiness.
Whitlock has asserted that "spiritual holiness or emotional
wholeness can be achieved only when the total self is involved.
Neither holiness nor wholeness will be secured if the self remains segmented. . . ."[8] Deficits of ontological givens result
in brokenness and stress. Not only are they a departure from
the ways things were meant to be, but they create longings to
recover the intended experience of *shalom*. What were givens
before the Fall have become psychospiritual *deficits* for all
human beings. The more completely and consistently we experience these essentials, the greater the levels of well-being
we experience.

Several contemporary secular psychologists who do not believe in Creation refer to similar fundamental states of being
or human need. Erich Fromm has suggested that human beings have four basic needs: rootedness, identity, transcendence,
and relation.[9] James Bugental asserts that human beings find
themselves in a "thrown condition" and struggle with existential anxiety and a continuing struggle to come to grips with
the realities of human existence. He has postulated five conditions of being:

1. Embodiedness—possessing a physical existence in time
   and space.

2. Finiteness—the awareness that we cannot know everything that determines a particular event and its
   consequences even though we may be affected.

3. The potential to act—the ability to affect the external
   world as well as our own inner perspectives.

4. Choice—a sense of limited autonomy and being more
   than merely instinctual beings.

5. Separateness—knowing that we are apart or different
   from others while in some measure desiring and being
   able to attach or bond ourselves to others.[10]

The human struggle involves accepting these conditions and
finding ways to work with them so that we are not immersed in
dread and dis-ease.

Abraham Maslow constructed a theoretical hierarchy of human need that also parallels some of these ontological givens.[11]
Maslow theorized that our most fundamental need is the need
for physiological survival. This is followed by needs for safety
or security, belongingness and love, self-esteem, and self-
actualization.

Theologian Paul Tillich proposed three main sources of existential anxiety that correspond to the premise that stress
results from psychospiritual deficits. These are the threat of
death and fate (roughly comparable to issues of equity and
transcendence), the experience of guilt and condemnation (related to deficits of acceptance and equity), and confronting

emptiness and meaninglessness (compatible with the deficits of significance and transcendence).[12] Bugental has further suggested that Tillich implies a fourth source of existential anxiety—the threat of isolation and loneliness.[13]

Recently, Christian psychologist Peter Schreck suggested that every person must come to terms with four relational life tasks: identity, intimacy, industry (related to the ontological notion of competence), and integrity (completeness, spirituality, related to the psychospiritual concepts of transcendence and *shalom*).[14]

THE FALL

According to the Bible, Satan approached Adam and Eve as part of his continuing warfare against God.[15] His seductive offer was aimed at their strong point—the ability to choose. Choice is perhaps the most godlike quality of human beings. It leads us to the heights of hope or the depths of despair. Human choice reflects the sovereignty of God, who is free to choose whatever he wishes without boundaries and limitations. It was Lucifer's rebellion against his exalted but finite state of boundedness that led to his fall. He appealed to exactly the same desire to be free of boundaries and the restrictions of finitude (to "be like God," Gen. 3:5) in Eve and Adam.

Once the fateful choices were made, the consequences of finite humanity's attempt to play sovereign God were immediately experienced. Figure 2.4 illustrates the spiritual, relational, and psychological brokenness and chaos introduced into human experience by sin. First, mankind's relationship with God was shattered and alienation resulted. Initially Adam and Eve had intimate, personal fellowship with him. Now, "the LORD God banished him from the Garden of Eden" (Gen. 3:23), and mankind has ever since been naturally alienated from the very One who could meet human needs. Second, the relationship of perfect intimacy, trust, and love between Adam and Eve was broken. Human beings began to experience isolation. What had been intended to be good (working together and bearing children) was now bad (struggle, domination, and pain).[16] Finally, the unified or authentic True Self, which perfectly reflected

After the Fall

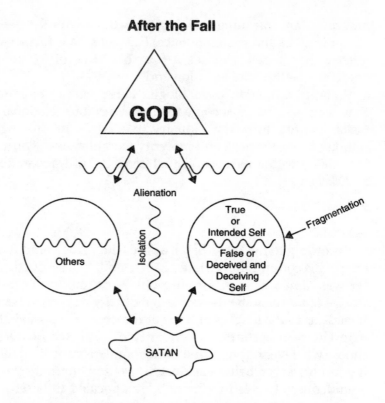

Fig. 2.4. Spiritual, interpersonal, and psychological brokenness were the result of the Fall.

God's image, became a divided self characterized by fragmentation, with the True Self and False Self at war with one another. What is left of our True (rational) Self made in the image of God is locked into conflict with our False (irrational) Self. The False Self is twisted with egocentricity and irrationality. It is responsive to deception, distortions, and condemnation. The True Self continues to struggle for "truth in the inward parts" (Ps. 51:6 KJV) and for the faith to believe in the elevated view of human worth consistently displayed by God's words and actions toward humanity. It is the part of the self that stretches toward health and holiness.

As a result of the Fall and subsequent sin choices by one's (False) self or others, disorder, distortion, disturbance, dysfunction, disintegration, and distress have consistently marred human experience. From the point of the Fall on, human experience has been primarily filled with distress and pain, rather than peace and joy. It is important to note that *distress and pain are alien to human nature. They are not what God intended for human beings to experience.* This is clearly demonstrated by Adam and Eve in their use of ego-defense mechanisms of denial, blaming, and deception. These ego defenses were aimed at countering their painful sense of responsibility for the chaos and catastrophe that resulted from their sin choices.

Due both to original sin transmitted through conception (see Ps. 51:5) and subsequent life choices, all human beings experience stress. Sin, *which is any choice or behavior that contradicts God's perfect design for humanity*, produces stress in several ways. First, as a result of the disorder introduced into the original creation, sin created a context of stress that we all live in. Romans 8:20–21 remarks that the "creation was subjected to frustration, not by its own choice, but by the will of the one who subjected it, in hope that the creation itself will be liberated from its bondage to decay and brought into the glorious freedom of the children of God." Second, the sin of others toward us as they fail to meet our psychospiritual needs and interact with us in ways that contradict love creates deepened distress. Third, our own sin choices and yielding to the temptation for immediate relief from stress worsen our long-term experience of distress.

Since the Fall, painful experiences of rejection and shame, loneliness, inadequacy (failure), victimization and exploitation, confusion and emptiness, anxiety, worthlessness, and meaninglessness have plagued human beings (see Figure 2.5). These contradictions of God-intended ontological givens become psychospiritual needs that motivate humans. We instinctively long for our psychospiritual needs to be met and for our pain to be relieved. The human journey is one of trying to avoid, escape from, minimize and manage the pain and stress of psychospiritual deficits and to experience the *shalom* of the originally sinless True Self. However, because we live in a post-Fall world and make sinful choices ourselves, this is only partially possible.

The Pain Released by Existential Deficits

A deficit of:	Leads to the pain of:
acceptance	rejection, shame
belonging	isolation
competence	inadequacy
equity	victimization
identity	confusion
security	anxiety
significance	worthlessness
transcendence	meaningless, chaos

Fig. 2.5

In essence, though, all human beings attempt to recover the blissful state of well-being Adam and Eve enjoyed in the pre-Fall Garden of Eden. The result of the Fall for humanity was the introduction of stress. Life is now a stressful process of scanning for acceptance, seeking for belonging, striving for competence, scrambling for equity, searching for identity, struggling for security, straining for significance, and stretching for transcendence. To the degree that our psychospiritual needs are met in ways consistent with God's guidelines for living, we experience well-being.

Unfortunately, our choices are often contradictory to God's design and ultimately make the pain worse. Depending upon which is more dominant, we are more or less healthy. We may lessen the pain of one ontological deficit by choosing a pattern that seems to work but that creates a deeper deficit in another area.

> *Sonya* came for counseling due to a growing sense of sadness. She found herself alternating between tears and anger for some undefinable reason. Only through counseling did it become clear that she had sacrificed a sense of healthy identity from early childhood in order to insure a place of acceptance and belonging. She had never felt her parents fully accepted her, so she had given up her self in order to try to win their approval. When they began clearly favoring another sister's child

and treating her son like he was inferior, strong feelings began to emerge. She had surrendered her identity for acceptance and belonging but ended up without either.

Larry tried to overcome deep feelings of loneliness (need to belong) by becoming a superachieving workaholic (need for competence). Through his work success he was able to feel like he was wanted and belonged (on the surface), but his deeper needs for intimacy were not being met. Consequently he became involved with several work-related affairs. The emotional and sexual intensity of the affairs made him feel like he finally had the closeness he desired, but their transience, the guilt, and the inevitable distancing from his wife only drove his loneliness deeper.

These "neurotic choices"[17] of the irrational False Self are attempts to overcome the uncertainties of the fallen and finite existence with levels of control and certainty that belong only to God. They contradict God's design for meeting psychospiritual needs generated by ontological deficits and result in the development of greater distress over time.

NOTES

1. See Craig W. Ellison and Joel Smith, "Toward an Integrative Measure of Health and Well-being," *Journal of Psychology and Theology* 19, no.1 (Spring 1991):35–48, for a more extensive discussion of the psychological and theological support for holism as the preferred and most healthy human state of being.

2. R. L. Harris, G. L. Archer, and B. K. Waltke, eds., *Theological Wordbook of the Old Testament*, vol. 2 (Chicago: Moody, 1980).

3. G. Kittel, ed., *Theological Dictionary of the New Testament*, trans. and ed., Geoffrey W. Bromiley, vol. 2 (Grand Rapids: Eerdmans, 1964).

4. D. W. Stacey, *The Pauline View of Man* (London: MacMillan, 1956).

5. Ray S. Anderson, *On Being Human: Essays in Theological Anthropology* (Grand Rapids: Eerdmans, 1982).

6. J. K. Howard, "The Concept of the Soul in Psychology and Religion," *Journal of the American Scientific Affiliation* 24 (1972): 151.

7. For research supporting this, see Ellison and Smith, "Health and Well-Being."

8. Glenn E. Whitlock, "The Structure of Personality in Hebrew Psychology," in *Wholeness and Holiness*, ed. H. Newton Malony (Grand Rapids: Baker, 1983), 41–51. (Reprinted from *Interpretation* 14 [1960]: 3–13.)

9. Erich Fromm, "Value, Psychology and Human Existence," in *New Knowledge in Human Values*, ed. A. H. Maslow (New York: Harper and Row, 1959), 151–64.

10. James F. T. Bugental, *The Search for Authenticity*, rev. ed. (New York: Irvington, 1981), 445.

11. Abraham Maslow, *Motivation and Personality*, 2d ed. (New York: Harper and Row, 1970), 37–58.

12. Paul Tillich, *The Courage to Be* (New Haven: Yale University Press, 1952).

13. James F. T. Bugental, *The Search for Authenticity* (New York: Holt, Rinehart, and Winston, 1965), 285.

14. G. Peter Schreck, "Personhood and Relational Life Tasks: A Model for Integrating Psychology and Theology," in *Family Therapy: Christian Perspectives*, ed. Hendrika Vande Kempe (Grand Rapids: Baker, 1991), 77–108.

15. See Craig W. Ellison, "The War of the Ages," unpublished manuscript.

16. Jeffrey Thompson, (Unpublished communication, July 1990).

17. Bugental, *Search for Authenticity*, 41–42.

Chapter Three

Growing Up Stressed

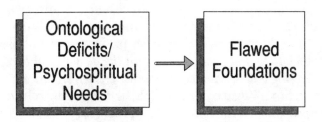

MENTAL AND EMOTIONAL DISTRESS AMONG CHILDREN is at alarming
levels in the United States. As many as 12 percent of the children under age eighteen (approximately 7.5 million) suffer
from some form of mental or emotional illness. Hospitaliza-
tions of young people for psychiatric disorders increased by
almost 50 percent during the last decade. The proportion of
children who have received counseling for emotional problems
also rose by over 50 percent during the 1980s. Suicides among
fifteen- to nineteen-year-olds have tripled during the last thirty
years. As many as 30 percent of children *under eighteen months*
of age have significant emotional difficulties.[1]

The amount of stress that a person experiences as an adult
and the healthy or unhealthy patterns used to manage stress
throughout life are largely established during childhood.
Childhood experiences produce a personality that is more or
less stress-prone. For some, childhood creates a deep reservoir
of residual stress. For others, a climate of caring love and

positive experiences fill the child with a sense of well-being. In both cases, children learn characteristic patterns of how to process and cope with the distress of life. Each person develops a unique blend of disposition, self-perception, ego defenses, values, emotions, behaviors, and controlling beliefs that affects his or her experience of stress throughout life. Each person's personality and behavior pattern represents the attempt to find solutions for the pain of psychospiritual distress.

Lynn was not expected to handle basic responsibilities of everyday living as a child. She never learned how to order her life. As an adult, she lives a highly chaotic and disorganized life, which exposes her to constant stress.

Stan learned to view himself as inadequate and incompetent, unable to deal successfully with the demands of life. His domineering and overprotective mother created significant self-doubt in Stan. While he is very fatalistic about being constantly swamped and overwhelmed by the stormy seas of life, he is also filled with deep rage and distress.

Saundra learned as a child that to assure acceptance by others she should not make people unhappy. As a result, she is an extremely nonassertive person who is constantly asked to do things beyond her job description or real desire. Although she complies very willingly, she has begun to develop severe migraine headaches and dread about going to work.

Adult stress is partially the result of (1) the amount and kind of stress experienced during childhood and (2) faulty learning that instills patterns of coping with pain that increase stress.

There is no way to predict which childhood stressors will deepen which ontological deficits. However, extreme stress results in more extensive disintegration of the ability to cope. It triggers severe anxiety and overwhelms the ability of the child to adjust. As a result, traumatic events usually have a long-term negative impact. This is due to conditioning, the creation of self-doubt, and faulty patterns of pain relief.

When stress impacts a child is also significant. Young children are most susceptible to long-term problems with stress because they have fewer options available to help them adjust.

For example, preschool children respond to parental divorce differently than do older children and adolescents.[2]

BIOLOGICAL INFLUENCES

PRENATAL STRESS

Several prenatal factors have significant negative effects on the ability of children to process and manage the stress of life. For example, each year approximately 250,000 infants in the United States are born seriously underweight. They are as much as three times more likely to be born blind, deaf, or mentally retarded. Approximately 200,000 cocaine-addicted babies are now born each year in the United States. Infants born to alcohol-, cigarette-, and drug-using mothers experience higher levels of physical and emotional stress than babies of mothers who abstain. Early reports indicate that prenatal use of the even more powerful drug "ice" by mothers leads to infants and children who are emotionally and socially nonresponsive; they appear unable to respond with normal social and moral sensitivity. Finally, severe and prolonged maternal stress during pregnancy may produce cleft palates, harelips, and other malformations.

Heredity also affects a person's sensitivity to stress. Nine levels of temperamental differences have been identified. These are activity level, rhythmicity, approach-withdrawal behavior, adaptability, intensity of reaction, threshold of responsiveness, quality of mood, distractibility, and attention span/persistence.[3] These characteristics persist through at least the first ten years of life. Higher levels of stress are experienced to a chronic degree by children who are not distractible, who withdraw in the face of new stimuli, who are less adaptive, who have short attention span/persistence, intense reactions, and a negative quality of mood.

BIOSOCIAL STRESSORS

Biosocial stressors include physical defects, serious injuries, illness, and physical assault. At least part of the stress is due to the reactions of other people. For example, people often have a difficult time relating normally and positively to a child who has a serious cleft palate or has suffered extensive facial burns. The child with these kinds of problems experiences greater levels of rejection, isolation, anxiety, and worthlessness than a beautiful, blue-eyed blonde. Severe disabling and malformation of body parts also increase stress due to the added energy required just to carry out life functions.

Serious injuries and illness include spinal cord injuries, burns, cancer, and other potentially fatal, debilitating, or disfiguring biological trauma. Among the immediate reactions a child has to acute injury or illness are anxiety, regression, depression, fear of bodily mutilation, belief that God is punishing them, and delays in normal perceptual-motor development.

The typical process of adaptation to acute injury or illness involves impact, recoil, and restitution.[4] The impact phase may last for several weeks and includes heavy denial, fantasy, regression, preoccupation with one's body, and strong needs for nurturance. The recoil phase involves mourning over the loss of self-potential due to the injury or illness and attempts to regain some sense of control over one's world. This phase may last for several months. There may be serious depression and interpretation of the illness as punishment for wrongdoing. Both of these phases require significant emotional support from parents and loved ones. If these two phases are successfully worked through, the child will enter restitution. This involves increasing acceptance of the illness/injury outcome and the altered future, as well as acceptance of one's altered self(body)-image. If the child does not make restitution, he or she will live life with substantial residual stress.

In addition to injury or illness itself, hospitalization and surgery create significant stress. For young children under age four, separation from parents usually produces anxiety, regression, sleep disruption, appetite disturbances, and ongoing problems with trust and autonomy.[5]

> *Leon was deathly ill as an infant of seven months. His illness and prolonged hospitalization resulted in separation each night from his mother and in touch-deprivation, because she was not able to hold him much. Throughout his teens and early*

adult life he has struggled with loneliness and depression rooted in this early disruption of the bonding process.

Long-term effects of hospitalization are most negative with young children. More than one hospitalization before four years of age is correlated with greater risk of behavior disturbances during childhood, learning difficulties and enuresis in adolescence, and depression and chronic pain in adulthood.[6]

School-age children are less threatened by separation. However, they often express fears that they are being punished and show anxiety over loss of body control as a result of their illness or injuries. Adolescents are more focused on body image and the possibility of death.

For all age groups, surgery evokes anxiety about body integrity and damage to body parts. Anxiety, panic, denial, passivity, and regression are common preoperative stresses.

Physical assault is a third traumatic biosocial stressor in childhood. This includes serious beatings, extreme neglect, incest, and rape. In fact, simply observing the effects of violence or living in a climate where violence is regularly feared produces stress.[7] Among the stress-induced effects of physical assault are anxiety, fear, withdrawal, shame, guilt, self-blame, low self-esteem, repressed rage, depression, antisocial behavior (acting out) and poor impulse control, preoccupation with sexual matters, violence, lack of trust, and sexually focused play. These feelings are usually chronic and last into adulthood. Sexual assault during childhood typically produces adult sexual dysfunctions, promiscuity, transient/negative relationships, and repeat victimization.[8]

GENDER

Another biologically based factor that more indirectly influences the experience of stress is gender. Males and females experience stress differently.[9] It appears that hormonal differences may produce variations in response to stress. Also, there are differences in the types of stressors experienced by males and females. Finally, role expectations are learned throughout childhood that result in different experiences and patterns of stress. Girls often learn to be passive, helpless, trusting, accepting, subordinate, meek, caretaking, and obedient. They frequently identify and express their emotions more openly and thoroughly than boys.

On the other hand, boys learn toughness, nonexpression of feelings, and action rather than communication. They are not usually encouraged to identify and express deeper levels of emotion. Instead, they are taught to deny and stuff emotions, to put on a tough exterior, ridicule feelings, or to condense feelings into an umbrella emotion such as anger (which is allowed but certainly does not help stress management in close relationships!). Their relationships are focused on activity rather than talk and upon competition rather than cooperation. As a result, feelings are threatening (stressors) to countless men who do not know what to do with them. Many men deny their feelings because they would rather be rational and deal with cold, hard facts. The result of these childhood socialization patterns is the creation of fractured, stress-filled relationships between countless husbands and wives.

PSYCHOSOCIAL INFLUENCES

Psychospiritual distress is the result of violations of our fundamental being. When we do not experience life as God intended, we experience distress. The pain or stress that we experience comes from feedback that intentionally or accidentally negates one or more of our ontological givens. Developmental influences that trigger negative experiences of rejection, isolation, incompetence, victimization, confusion, anxiety, worthlessness, and boredom/emptiness create stress.

The more loving and affirming our family and peer relationships are, the more likely we will experience *shalom* and enter adulthood with relatively low levels of residual stress. The more depriving and dysfunctional our family system is, the greater our experience of immediate and long-term (residual) stress. Home environments that are relatively stable, consistent, sensitive, affirming, caring, gentle, and loving produce the greatest levels of well-being.

Pathogenic family systems, abuse/neglect, divorce, and death are major influences that create extensive and intensive stress that may last a lifetime. Their negative impact is extensive because they create ontological deficits and produce psycho-spiritual distress in several areas at one time. As a result, a child may feel simultaneously rejected, isolated, victimized, confused, anxious, and worthless.

PATHOGENIC FAMILY SYSTEMS

Pathogenic family systems use distorted patterns and rules of interaction. These patterns include rejection/scapegoating, overprotection and restrictiveness, unrealistic demands, overpermissiveness and indulgence, faulty discipline, inadequate and irrational communication, and undesirable models.[10] Each of these patterns generates long-term stress by giving feedback that creates ontological deficits, enhances twisted self-perception, and promotes dysfunctional ways of dealing with emotional pain.

Rejection and scapegoating are communicated by parents who verbally or nonverbally indicate that they wish a child had not been born, show that they cannot tolerate central attributes of a child, or make a child the primary focus of blame for much of what goes wrong in the family.

> *It took forty-year-old* **Vernon** *about two years in therapy before he finally understood and was able to constructively deal with the many ways in which his mother and older brothers constantly scapegoated him. He grew up with the feeling that he was inferior and that he existed only to serve them. Because he was somewhat like his despised and divorced father, he was somehow a "bad" person who could only become "good" by doing what his mother and brothers wanted from him. What they wanted was often at great cost to him and his family, and he never was given the approval he hoped for.*

Rejection is often triggered by verbal and nonverbal messages that one is different, not wanted, weird, or bad. Maternal indifference and rejection lead to short-term failure to thrive and long-term physical, mental, and emotional disorders.[11] Feelings of rejection, guilt, and shame are fostered by a variety of nonnurturing interactions by parents. These include failing to respond to an infant's needs in a timely and appropriate

way, not holding the child, not emotionally and verbally interacting with the baby or toddler, harsh discipline, verbal abuse,
indifference, coldness, refusal to pay attention, perfectionism,
criticism, self-absorption, constant criticism, lack of interest in
the child's activities, failure to respect the child's viewpoint
and feelings, and threats to get rid of the child. Rejection is associated with aggression, excessive fears, lying and stealing,
and a wide variety of psychological disorders in adolescence
and adulthood.[12]

> *Shirley was raised by a mother who never expressed any
> form of pleasure or affirmation to her. Rather, she pointed out
> ways that Shirley should be more like her older sister, work
> harder, do better. Even as an adult, Shirley feels like she can
> never please her mother and that her parents regard her exist-
> ence as a bother.*

Peers may create significant stress through rejection as well.

> *Larry felt like an outsider from the time he moved into a
> new neighborhood in the sixth grade. The other kids made fun
> of his accent, beat him up whenever they could catch him on the
> way home from school, called him a sissy, and refused to select
> him for their teams at school. He was under such extreme stress
> that he cried to not go to school, could not eat and lost weight,
> and could not do his homework. He eventually found some kids
> in his neighborhood who acted friendly toward him. The prob-
> lem was that they were already using drugs and were into
> pornography. In order to be accepted, Larry joined in and be-
> came addicted to both. By the time he was seventeen he had been
> arrested for his drug use and had fathered children by two dif-
> ferent girls.*

Peer rejection is not always this severe, of course, but the
stress generated over the issue of peer acceptance is significant
for most adolescents, and especially for those who are already
insecure due to dysfunctional home environments.

Peer value systems create stress when they contradict God's
design for human health or conflict with parental/familial values.

Jerry found himself under tremendous stress due to value conflict between his familial values and those of the group he wanted to be accepted by. The group valued drinking and partying, and placed a high emphasis on materialism and "doing your own thing." This was in marked contrast to the conservative values of his Christian family and caused Jerry to experience intense inner struggles, which led to several trips to the doctor for gastro-intestinal complaints.

Overprotection and restrictiveness produce doubts about one's ability to competently face life, dependency, repressed hostility, and extreme anxiety.

Freida was constantly told by her grandmother and mother to be careful and was given the verbal and nonverbal message that men might do something bad to her. They read newspaper clippings to her to support their cautions. She was not allowed to play at other children's homes or to be involved in after-school activities. There was considerable concern that she eat properly and get enough sleep. When she hurt herself or got sick, she was given a clear message that it was her fault, that her mother had done everything possible to protect her. As an adult Freida developed a full-blown obsessive-compulsive disorder involving fear of possible contamination by AIDS. She felt highly vulnerable and susceptible to invasion by this dreaded disease, engaging in a variety of compulsive behaviors designed to prevent her from contracting it and then being blamed. Her daily life was saturated with stress.

Lois was a victim of parents who made unrealistic demands upon her. At the age of six she was expected to thoroughly clean the house each week. By age ten she had to fix breakfast and dinner for the four people in her family. In junior high school she was expected to continue those responsibilities and to get nothing but A's in school. By ninth grade she was expected to have a job as well in order to help out her parents, who were both alcoholics. Unrealistic demands lead to problems with negative self-perception, false guilt, fear of failure, shame and self-condemnation, codependency, and perfectionism.

Doug's alcoholic mother was never satisfied with his per-formance. Before his father died when he was an early teen, he got very little attention from either parent. After his father's death, his mother became totally self-absorbed. Douglas became an outstanding musician, hoping that he could somehow be so good that she would have to notice and approve. She didn't, but others did. However, as Doug grew older and became a pro-fessional musician he struggled with severe anxiety rooted in the fear that he would do something such as fainting during a performance that would publicly shame him.

Overpermissive and indulgent parents cater to their child's slightest whims and rarely say "no." This is often the result of guilt due to parental absence from the home because of work demands. It may also relate to the parents' desire to be liked by their children or to be free of cumbersome parental respon-sibilities. While this style of parenting may not produce problems initially, a child's subsequent adjustment to the out-side world is often problematic and can result in significant stress.

Faulty discipline includes practices that are either too harsh, too lenient, or inconsistent. Inconsistent discipline creates con-fusion, making it difficult for a child to develop healthy and stable values. Inconsistent discipline is clearly related to sub-sequent delinquent or criminal behavior.[13] Discipline that is too permissive creates difficulties with self-control, insecurity, and aggressiveness. Discipline that is too harsh crushes initiative, promotes anxiety, hinders development of positive self-esteem, and leads to excessive preoccupation with keeping or break-ing rules.

Inadequate and irrational communication includes not listening and giving support during crises, distortion or disconfirmation of intended meanings, and contradiction or undermining of a child's experiences and conclusions.

Frank was never allowed to express any kind of negative emotion. If he tried to do so, he was told that he was just tired, or that somehow he was mistaken to think such things and that he was probably misunderstanding what really had happened.

The results of such faulty communication patterns tend to be feelings of rejection, self-doubt, identity confusion, worthlessness, and victimization.

Finally, pathogenic parents are *models of unhealthy and stress-filled living* because they have faulty assumptions about reality, overdepend on defense mechanisms, engage in self-defeating (neurotic) or psychotic behavior, are involved in substance abuse or crime, excessively blame and shame, refuse to face and deal with their problems, or lie and cheat. Children in these families usually adopt these patterns because they are emotionally bonded to their parents and do not know any other way.

ABUSE/NEGLECT

Arnold entered counseling in a highly stressed condition. Recently engaged, he was concerned about his ability to be a good husband and father. Arnold was raised in a Christian home by a highly aggressive father and a highly passive mother. His father typically worked twelve- to fourteen-hour days. Throughout his childhood Arnold was disciplined harshly by his father, who would fly into a rage at minor infractions. In therapy he learned that being punched, kicked, and beaten severely were physical abuse, not discipline.

In addition to the physical abuse, Arnold was subjected to verbal ridicule by his peers and his parents for being "dumb." He was frequently humiliated for his school failure. He learned as a teenager that he was dyslexic.

During the course of his therapy, he discovered that he had adopted a pattern of workaholism similar to his father's in an attempt to prevent failure; he was obsessed with being a success and avoiding failure. He also learned that his anger was rooted in the victimization he had experienced at his father's hands, and that his anger was activated whenever he felt he was being humiliated.

It is estimated by the National Center on Child Abuse and Neglect that over one million children are abused or neglected each year. As many as 200,000 of these are physically abused, and as many as 100,000 are sexually abused; the remainder are neglected.

Incestuous relationships and childhood sexual abuse produce depression, anger, fear/anxiety, guilt/shame, difficulty trusting and establishing relationships, repeated victimization, shutting off or overcontrolling of emotions, sexual problems in marriage, and poor self-image in those who have been violated.[14]

Sexual, physical, and emotional abuse create lifelong stress as a result of an intricate interplay between ego-defense mechanisms and controlling lies. These victims have considerable difficulty trusting another person, because those who are close have betrayed them. This leads to difficulty in forming and maintaining friendships and intimate relationships.[15] These are lonely people. Often they are not able to face or reveal their deep inner wounds but the pain seeps out in a variety of destructive ways.

> *Joann, a victim of sexual abuse when she was eleven, found herself being highly critical of her husband (as her stepfather had been of her), suspicious of him, and uninterested in normal marital intimacy.*
>
> *Bob seemed to be overcome by almost uncontrollable rage and a strong urge to physically abuse his three-year-old son when he got whiny or did not obey immediately. During therapy he realized that his father had battered him whenever he somehow bothered the father and was not good.*
>
> *Leila shut down emotionally and was unable to communicate feelings to her husband or to enjoy normal marital intimacy. She was locked in an emotional prison for twenty years of her marriage, until she began to uncover traumatic experiences. Before she was ten she had been the victim of incest by her grandfather and was raped by two boys. As she was able to face these traumatic experiences and talk about them with her husband, her depression lessened, and she was able to begin risking other feelings with him.*

Emotional abuse includes being cursed, verbally put down, ignored, screamed at, and other interactions that devalue a child. Emotionally abused children struggle with shame, damaged self-esteem, depression, and the belief that there is something wrong with them. They are usually withdrawn, apathetic, overly rigid in conforming to instructions from adult authority figures, and experience behavior problems.[16]

DIVORCE OR DEATH

Divorce has significant and negative emotional effects on children. These children struggle with chronic feelings of anger, depression, insecurity, rejection, guilt, identity confusion, and loneliness. As adults, they have increased vulnerability to stress, more anxiety regarding future relationships, lower self-esteem, greater feelings of being overwhelmed, problems relating to people, higher divorce rates, and difficulty expressing emotions in a mature way.[17] While approximately 20 percent of all American children have developmental, learning, or emotional problems, children from single-parent families and families with stepparents are two to three times more likely to have emotional problems and learning disabilities.[18] One of the most significant outcomes is the "sleeper effect."[19] This includes the emergence of depression, fears and anxieties about committing to a marriage, and sexual promiscuity during late adolescence or early adulthood. The sleeper effect seems to hit girls harder than boys.

Children of divorce frequently develop feelings of inadequacy and self-doubt. As a result of their damaged self-image, they tend to be more perfectionistic and struggle more than children from healthy, intact families with insecurity, control, fear of risk, fear of intimacy, anger, depression, inadequate self-boundaries, and paralysis of initiative in relationships and work.[20]

Death of a parent is a traumatic event as well. It often leads to long-term difficulties with insecurity, guilt, and loneliness. Even prolonged parent absence due to job requirements can create subsequent difficulties.

Eileen came from a home where her father was gone for six months at a time due to his maritime employment. Her mother was very self-sufficient and competent and did not seem to need her husband. When Eileen married, she discovered that she had strong feelings of jealousy toward her husband and

*demanded that he spend considerable time at home. At the same
time, she was very controlling and left him feeling so emascu-
lated that he began to have trouble functioning sexually. He felt
overwhelmed by her and wanted space, but she became highly
upset when he tried to pull away enough to even fulfill his basic
work responsibilities.*

SPIRITUAL STRESSORS

Developmental stress may also come from several spiritual
sources. These include the sin of others against the child, sin
choices by the child, and spiritual experiences.

When others act toward a child in ways that contradict
God's design for healthy human relationships, stress is created.
Any behaviors that are unloving and damage a child's experience of acceptance, belonging, competence, equity, identity,
security, significance, or transcendence are sinful and generate
the stress that comes from the negation of the child's ontological givens. Words or actions that somehow communicate
rejection, shame, not being wanted, failure, exploitation, confusion of identity, anxiety, devaluation, or the futility of
existence generate ontological deficits. The experience of these
deficits is stressful. It leads to instinctive efforts by the highly
vulnerable child to reconcile the painful feedback that goes
against his intrinsic sense of being created as a worthwhile and
loved (by God) being.

Sometimes the sin of others is particularly intentional and
traumatic, as in the growing number of reported cases of satanic ritual abuse. Children subjected to the emotional, sexual,
physical, and spiritual trauma of ritual abuse may develop severe cases of multiple personality disorder as a way of trying
to cope with the overwhelming nature of the abuse.[21]

Early spiritual experiences in the home, church, or Chris-
tian/parochial school may create enduring spiritual stress.

*Margaret told how she felt so overwhelmed and afraid of
God as a result of her parents' cautions and the institutional
formality of her first communion in the Catholic church. She
has struggled as a born-again adult believer with a number of*

crippling emotions about the church and God, which seem to be
partially rooted in her early experiences of the church.

Others whom I have counseled have poured out stories of
how they felt shame and guilt about themselves as a result of
the spiritual teaching they received and the austere demeanor
(the face of God, as it were) that was expressed by Christian
authority figures. Parents who use God as a cosmic baby-sitter
and threaten his punishment as a way to control their children
set them up for a lifetime of distance and alienation from God.
These children experience considerable spiritual stress due to
their unhealthy fear of God and not having his loving support
emotionally accessible to them.

There are also increasing reports of childhood demonization
through the transmission of generational demons or through
exploration with the occult, drugs, and illicit sex. Supposedly
innocent games such as the Ouija™ board or the Dungeons and
Dragons™ game have been linked to demonization. Childhood demons encourage perception and patterns of behavior
that are distorted and ultimately destructive. Frequently they
so intertwine themselves with the child's personality that
adults experiencing deliverance from childhood demonization
fear that they will lose their identity and become an empty
void.

Finally, sin choices of a developing child/adolescent may
directly cause stress or shape unhealthy patterns of coping
with stress that in turn create longer-term disintegration. Ado-
lescent alcoholism, sexual acting out and promiscuity, heavy
metal music, and pornographic literature or videos are but a
few of the temptations that teens are likely to face.

<h3 style="text-align:center">SUMMARY</h3>

Mature, healthy personhood that has a maximum of well-
being and a minimum of stress depends largely upon the
experience of consistent love and nurturing during childhood.
A child who is exposed to extremely high levels of stress or learns
ways of dealing with pain that are distorted and destructive
will enter adulthood with a full reservoir of developmental

(residual) stress. Inadequate coping patterns learned in childhood will produce greater distress as they are used to face adult stress. All that is learned in childhood as a result of biological, psychospiritual, and spiritual experiences directly affects a person's lifelong experiences of distress and well-being. As a consequence of those influences, adults with greater residual stress from childhood are more likely to make destructive Downward Path choices and less likely to make constructive Upward Path choices. These choices and their consequences will be discussed in chapter 7.

NOTES

1. Kathleen Brady, Elizabeth Taylor, and James Willwerth, "Struggling for Sanity," *TIME* 8 October 1990, 47–48.

2. Richard A. Gardner, "Childhood Stress Due to Parental Divorce," in *Stressors and the Adjustment Disorders*, ed. Joseph D. Noshpitz and R. Dean Coddington (New York: Wiley, 1990), 43–59.

3. S. Chess, A. Thomas, and H. G. Birch, *Your Child Is a Person* (New York: Viking, 1965); A. Thomas and S. Chess, "Behavioral Individuality in Childhood," in *Development and Evolution of Behavior*, ed. L. R. Aronson et al. (San Francisco: Freeman, 1970); A. Thomas, and S. Chess, *Temperament and Development* (New York: Brunner-Mazel, 1977); A. Thomas and S. Chess, *The Dynamics of Psychological Development* (New York: Brunner-Mazel, 1980); A. Thomas, S. Chess, and H. G. Birch, *Temperament and Behavior Disorders in Children* (New York: New York University Press, 1968); A. Thomas, S. Chess, and H. G. Birch, "The Origin of Personality," *Scientific American* 223 (1970): 102–9.

4. D. G. Prugh and C. K. Taguiri, "Emotional Aspects of the Respirator Care of Patients with Poliomyelitis," *Psychosomatic Medicine* 42 (1954): 177–95.

5. Dane G. Prugh and Troy L. Thompson II, "Illness as a Source of Stress: Acute Illness, Chronic Illness, and Surgical Procedures," in *Stressors and the Adjustment Disorders*, ed. Noshpitz and Coddington, 60–142.

6. Ibid., 68.

7. Tori DeAngelis, "Living with Violence: Children Suffer, Cope," *APA Monitor* (January 1991): 26–27. Also, Lee Ann Hoff, *People in Crisis: Understanding and Helping* (Redwood City, Calif.: Addison-Wesley, 1989) has a helpful section on assisting victims of various forms of violence, across the developmental life span.

8. Kendall Johnson, *Trauma in the Lives of Children: Crisis and Stress Management Techniques for Counselors and Other Professionals* (Claremont, Calif.: Hunter House, 1989), 13–14.

9. Dorothy H. G. Cotton, *Stress Management: An Integrated Approach to Therapy* (New York: Brunner-Mazel, 1990), xv–xxi.

10. James C. Coleman, James N. Butcher, and Robert C. Carson, *Abnormal Psychology and Modern Life* (Glenview, Ill.: Scott Foresman, 1980), 144–52.

11. D. M. Bullard et al., "Failure to Thrive in the Neglected Child," *American Journal of Orthopsychiatry* 37 (1967): 680–90.

12. Coleman, Butcher, and Carson, *Abnormal Psychology*, 146.

13. Ibid., 149.

14. Jan Frank, *A Door of Hope: Recognizing and Resolving the Pains of Your Past* (San Bernardino, Calif.: Here's Life, 1987), 26–41.

15. Grant L. Martin, *Counseling for Family Violence and Abuse* (Dallas: Word, 1987), 132–33.

16. Ibid., 131, 139.

17. Kent McGuire, "Adult Children of Divorce: Curative Factors of Support Group Therapy" (doctoral research paper presented to the faculty of the Rosemead Graduate School of Psychology, Biola University, La Mirada, Calif., May 1987).

18. Peter Freiberg, "Study: Disorders Found in 20 Percent of Children," *APA Monitor* (February 1991): 36.

19. Judith S. Wallerstein and Sandra Blakeslee, *Second Chances: Men, Women and Children a Decade after Divorce* (New York: Ticknor and Fields, 1989), 56–64.

20. Jim Conway, *Adult Children of Legal or Emotional Divorce: Healing Your Long-Term Hurt* (Downers Grove, Ill.: InterVarsity, 1990), 55–69.

21. James G. Friesen, *Uncovering the Mystery of MPD* (San Bernardino, Calif.: Here's Life, 1991).

Chapter Four

Dispositional Distress

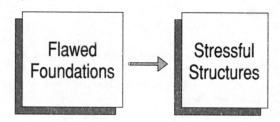

Any mother of several children will attest to the fact that each newborn baby is a unique being, with individual differences evident right at the beginning. Newborn infants show differences in responses to stimuli, general state of activity, and desire for touch and awareness. During childhood we build upon these innate differences and develop unique psychological structures and patterns of perceiving, processing, and responding to experience. These differences, which we can summarize as personality, either intensify or moderate the objective stress-value of potential stressors.

Some people encounter more stress in childhood or learn faulty ways of coping with experience. These people develop a defensive or distressed personality, which heightens the level of stress experienced throughout life.

Faulty learning is the primary process by which the characteristic patterns of personality, self-perception, shame, emotions, ego defenses, values, and gender responses are shaped and contribute to stress. Faulty learning may come through observation of others in the home or media, instruction from authority figures, trial and error, or conditioning. Faulty learning distorts a person's perception of the world and attempts to cope with distress. The result is that, for many, coping is marked by dysfunctional patterns of response to pain.

PERSONALITY

Personality structures and guides our experience of life in general ways. It consists of characteristics of a person that are generally consistent and predictable over time and across situations.

Although a particular personality trait may not play a key role in all cases of stress, it can become a source of vulnerability and dysfunction for a specific person.[1] It is apparently not stress per se that results in behavior problems among children, for example. The key is excessive stress due to poorness of fit between a child's temperament (personality) and the demands of the environment upon the child.

Three temperament constellations found in children are relevant to stress and adjustment disorders.[2] Some children typically respond to new stimuli positively, are very adaptable in response to change, and have a moderately intense mood-state that is mostly positive. At the opposite extreme are children who show negative withdrawal responses to most new stimuli, struggle with adaptation to change, and have generally negative and intense mood expressions. In the middle are children who show a combination of mildly negative responses to new stimuli and slow adaptability, even after repeated contact with those stimuli.

Hardiness is an important personality trait. It reflects an internal sense of control. Hardy persons see challenges as opportunities to stretch and grow. They do not see themselves as victims but believe that they are capable and competent. They have a proactive orientation toward life. They initiate action upon their world in order to promote well-being for themselves and for those they care about. They have an "I *can*" attitude. They are not gamblers, but they have a desire to experiment and experience new things. As a result, when new things come their way, they are less threatened and more likely to show flexible responses. They are resilient. Often, they seem to be people of faith. They have faith in themselves, faith that things will work out, and faith that God is in control and they will make it through.

In contrast, those who are vulnerable seem to feel and act like victims of life. They lack belief in their capacity to handle even the normal strains of living, and are blown out of the water by stressors that seem rather insignificant to the hardy person. These people often frequent a pastor's or counselor's office and telephone them with continual crises that are usually exaggerated. Their lives seem to be filled with tragedy and chaos.

Other personality characteristics that have been shown to be related to stress are dependency, Type A personality, hostility, and perfectionism. *Dependency* increases stress by making the dependent person highly sensitive and responsive to the moods and behaviors of at least one other person. Dependent people also are passive and see themselves as having little control over their life. They live defensive lives filled with fear that they will somehow upset those around them and experience some form of rejection.

Type A personality has been shown to increase both stress and heart disease,[3] although it appears that hostility is a critical element in that relationship. Recent research shows that cynical hostility (a mixture of hostility and mistrust) factors in higher blood pressure and cardiovascular disease.[4] The Type A person is generally competitive, plans too much to do in too little time, and tries to do several things at once.

Perfectionism both triggers and intensifies stress because of the underlying message that one cannot relax and be satisfied with the way one is or the way things are. The perfectionist feels that there is always more that should be done or changes that need to be made. Perfectionism refuses its owner permission to rest emotionally.

It is important to remember that a person's responses to a potential stressor reflect the interaction of these personality factors. Because of that, it is not likely that predictions of how a person will respond to potential stressors will be very accurate.

This is not particularly of concern, however, because the counselor's role is more retroactive. The counselor tries to sort out how particular personal predispositions have created or contributed to the counselee's stress perception and responses. Intervention is then aimed at altering personality patterns enough to reduce stress.

SELF-PERCEPTION/SELF-EVALUATION

An important component of personality is self-perception and self-evaluation. Self-perception is a product of the ways in which people think about themselves. No other creatures seem to be capable of viewing themselves as the object of their own thoughts. From the moment of birth, infants begin receiving information about who they are and how those around them feel about them.[5] These verbal and nonverbal messages from emotionally significant others are gradually organized into patterns and internalized. As internalization occurs, children begin to draw conclusions about themselves and make these their own. Over time these conclusions become controlling beliefs about one's self that either promote or moderate the experience of stress throughout life.

Self-perception is stable and does not change easily due to its early formation and grounding in emotionally based encounters with significant others. It does appear, however, that girls experience a larger drop in self-esteem during adolescence than boys.[6] Surprisingly, adult family members and educators impact girls' self-esteem the most through the transmission of expectations about their capacity to competently do various things.

Self-perception is highly important because it affects the processing of information that might be interpreted as stress, the residual stress within the person, and that person's responses to perceived stressors.

Stella felt that she was weird or different, though she was not really sure why. She had difficulty identifying anything that she liked about herself. Her family members always laughed her off and gave her the feeling that she was not worth paying serious attention to. She found it very hard to make decisions and *lived life passively, so she would not draw unnecessary atten-tion to herself. She had few friends and was lonely but somewhat stoical, as she felt that she did not really deserve to have friends. Stella felt constantly under pressure and frequently exploited by others. Life somehow just came **at** her, and she felt like what she did in response did*

What one believes about one's self and how one feels about one's self are significant factors in determining one's ability to adapt to the stresses of life.

Among the most stress-producing self-perceptions are

1. "Life is just too much for me." This magnifies the nor-mal wear and tear of life into overwhelming size and encourages a kind of fatalism whereby one's life is per-ceived to be totally at the mercy of outside forces.

2. "I'll never do anything right." This belief discourages setting and pursuing goals because of prophesied failure. The person who holds to this belief seldom experiences the esteem that comes from exercising dominion (com-petently managing one's life experience) and lives under the stress of negative anticipation.

3. "I'll never amount to anything (important)." If the one holding to this belief is actually still fighting against it, he or she may try to prove the belief wrong by such stress-generating patterns as workaholism. Workaholism creates its own direct stress but also tends to result in indirect stress as a result of negatively impacted close relationships. On the other hand, the person may give up and face the stresses of an irresponsible lifestyle.

Stress is not only related to how one perceives one's self but also to how one *feels* about his or her self-perception. Starting in infancy, children not only hear language applied to them by others but, even more importantly, begin to sense how others *feel* about them. Feelings of being devalued or rejected form the faulty foundation of negative self-esteem. Negative self-esteem is stress-generating.

The basis of self-esteem for most people in Western society is social comparison. That is, we are measured from infancy by others, and we subsequently measure ourselves throughout life on the basis of how we compare with others in relation to certain prized values. In Western society physical attractiveness, productivity, possessions, and power are among the most valued characteristics. We are led to believe that we are worth more the better we look, the more athletic we are, the greater our achievements, the more we own, and the more power we have. The problem is that these qualities are both comparative and transient. There is no absolute standard of having "made it." Neither is there any long-term stability with any of these values. As a result, those who build their sense of self-worth on the foundation of these values are not able to relax and just *be* themselves. Instead, they are always having to struggle with their own aging process, set and accomplish higher goals, look out for possible competition, and continually expend effort to maintain their conditional self-esteem. The result is a stress-saturated society filled with anxious, distressed, and self-doubting people who have great difficulty relaxing and accepting themselves as they are.

SHAME

Perhaps the most distressing disposition is a shame-based self. Shame is the bedrock belief that one is bad or defective at the core of one's being. It is the feeling of being irretrievably "no good" or "not good enough." Shamed people often perceive themselves as incompetent, unwanted, pitiful, nothing, deserving of criticism, and weak.[7] The failure to accept and value one's self is at the heart of shame.

Shame sticks to a person's identity like crazy glue. It creates and intensifies stress for several reasons. The pervasive self-doubt of a shamed personality not only plagues the person but also stimulates unhealthy attempts to silence the shame. These dysfunctional attempts include workaholism, codependency, perfectionism, addictions, and promiscuity. These patterns are deceptive because they generate stress while giving the immediate perception of relieving it.

Shame also encourages a person to interpret all difficulties and problems as deserved judgment for one's essential badness.

This kind of thinking promotes passivity and fatalism toward life. Questions about one's spiritual destiny (Is God going to punish me forever in hell?) frequently arise in this context. Living with a continuing sense of condemnation is highly stressful. Shame promotes the belief that one does not have the capacity to be competent, which triggers the chronic stress of self-doubt.

Because shame carries with it a deep feeling of rejection, it often sensitizes the person to any interactions that may be interpreted as rejection. The cost of such constant vigilance is more stress. Furthermore, shame encourages a person to avoid emotionally close relationships. This is due to anxiety over anticipated rejection if the other person really got to know the shame-filled individual. Shame frequently leads, therefore, to a deep-seated fear of abandonment and loneliness, which wrestles with the competing fear of rejection. The result is that many shame-based people are paralyzed with stress. They are afraid of getting close to another while at the same time wanting somehow to get close to someone in order to relieve their anxiety over possible isolation.

Finally, many who are shame-based feel extremely vulnerable. Repeated invasions of their personal space have left them feeling like they are not respected as persons and do not have (sometimes, do not have the right to) an identity of their own. As a result, they struggle with anxiety and feelings of violation due to chronic invasion of personal boundaries by family members and others who are more domineering and controlling.

> *Daphne is a sweet and conscientious person who will bend over backwards to help others. When she entered therapy with her husband due to some church-related problems, she indicated that she was very depressed. She felt like she was constantly trying—and failing—to be the perfect Christian mother for their three-year-old daughter, Jenny. She and her husband felt increasing resentment over what seemed to be her parents' attempts to undermine Daphne and Don's parenting of Jenny. Her parents excused Jenny's misbehavior in her presence while subtly criticizing Daphne and Don's standards. Her parents repeatedly involved Jenny in activities that made her want to stay with them after Daphne and Don came to pick her*

up and indicated they had to leave immediately. The result was that Jenny was pulled in two directions and had increasing temper tantrums.

The mere mention of her father in our therapy sessions resulted in tears coming to Daphne's eyes. She remembered constant messages from him, such as, "Kids are a burden." Daphne felt she was not wanted and was regarded as bad throughout her childhood. She remembered when she was ten years old wanting to kill herself by choking herself with one of her Dad's ties. She never trusted her father and did not want to be alone with him because somehow she was afraid he would do something bad. She did no think he had physically abused her, but he was emotionally cold toward her. Her mother did not demonstrate love and affection toward her either. This feeling of rejection was repeatedly reaffirmed after Jenny's birth. While her parents fawned over Jenny, her father usually ignored Daphne and pointedly told her that she would not be able to touch a trust fund he had established for Jenny.

As a very young teen Daphne was forced to work to provide for all of her needs, including clothes. As a result of feeling pushed out of her home, she got very involved with boys and with alcohol, becoming a borderline alcoholic.

Daphne realized that she had internalized such parental messages as "Don't upset Mom or Dad (especially Dad)." This had generalized to "Don't upset people," and "Don't upset God." As a result she became a people-pleaser.

During the course of therapy, Daphne became extremely anxious. When fixing the second of two major dinners for family members on Christmas Eve and Christmas Day, she became obsessed with worries about whether she had contaminated the food she had prepared so that her parents would get sick. In order to allay her anxiety, she began washing her hands about twenty times each day. Upon reflection in counseling, she realized that she had been thinking, "Someone might get sick and die. If that happens, I'll be blamed. I can't do anything right. I'm not any good to anyone. What good am I?"

For a period of three months Daphne was intensely down on herself and blaming herself. She was extremely fearful of making mistakes and being punished by others or by God. This *coincided with her attempts to become more assertive and less intimidated by her parents. Gradually, the obsessive-compulsive behaviors decreased as she gained the insight that her hand-washing was related to self-condemnation over feeling inadequate and as she began to see her mother respond to her assertiveness with respect, if not affirmation. She began to realize that much of her anxiety was a form of punishing herself for violating sub-conscious rules that acted to keep her locked in shame. She wondered if her fear of making mistakes was because she felt like she was a mistake. She began to be freed as she realized that the negative thoughts and feelings were expressions of resistance to change by the shame-based False Self. As Daphne gradually was able to battle the shame and feel the benefits of being asser-tive, she moved past the condemning, obsessive-compulsive anxiety and felt new levels of self-esteem.*

Valerie is also a sweet woman who is shame-based and shackled by incredible self-doubt. She has struggled all her life with feelings of condemnation. She came into therapy feeling like she did not know who she was and like there was a big hole in her. During the course of therapy she realized she had great anger inside as she revealed horrifying fears that she might do terrible things to people she loved—especially her mother.

Valerie had learned such controlling beliefs as "Don't rock the boat," "A good daughter is responsible to make her parents happy," "Mother knows best," "To feel okay about myself I must feel accepted by my mother," and "I am responsible to take care of my parents forever." Neither of her parents were nasty, but Valerie's mother constantly questioned Valerie's decisions, criti-cized her husband, and whined and induced guilt about Valerie not paying enough attention to her. ("After all, I'm not going to be around forever, you know.") In this case, Valerie's shame was the product of an overly protective, domineering mother who ostensibly was only wanting to be close to her daughter and help her. The result, however, was the feeling of being owned by her mother, having no identity of her own, and constantly being invaded and invalidated.

Shame-based identities are the product of family systems that have vague or distorted personal boundaries, violate and diminish the personhood of (some or all) family members, and are perfectionistic, rejecting, punishing, and abandoning. They typically lack accountability, are rigid and unforgiving, and lack empathy.[8] Shame-encouraging parents often treat children as ego extensions and do not allow them to form their own separate and unique identities.[9] Mistakes are often occasions for demeaning comments and humiliation by other family members.

Lee was constantly ridiculed by his family and treated as retarded. It was not until therapy in his late twenties that he began to realize that he had considerable abilities. His leadership efforts to aid senior citizens in his church and community began to attract the positive attention of many in the town. As he courageously pushed ahead, shedding the image of being a crippled person and doing things his parents had discouraged him from trying, he began to gain self-respect, and his parents' views of him gradually changed as well.

Shame-stimulating families tend to discourage genuine intimacy and either smother or distance from their children. Standards are not consistently enforced; when they are enforced it is often very intense and physically harsh. Children in these families learn that they cannot depend on others to empathetically meet their personal needs. Parents in these families do not affirm their children for who they are or what they have contributed. Mistakes are emphasized instead. Members of these families live with nagging self-doubt, distrust of others, fear of abandonment, passive interaction patterns, and the conviction that somehow they are defective, bad, and to blame for life's inevitable problems. Stress indeed!

EMOTIONAL STATE

The emotional state of a person refers to the ongoing affective condition of the individual, as well as to his or her current state. Those suffering from more severe affective or mood disorders, such as depression, tend to process their world more darkly and see themselves as unable to cope with the stressors that enter their life. Ontological deficits tend to carry characteristic emotional expressions with them (see figure 4.1).

In addition to these more entrenched patterns, how one is feeling at the moment that a stressor is introduced will affect both appraisal and response to the stressor. A person who is highly agitated is, in effect, already in a state of stress. The effect of subsequent stressors is magnified by the preexisting turmoil.

Deficit-Generated Emotions and Patterns

Ontological deficit of:	Consequences:
Acceptance	Feelings of rejection, shame, depression. Patterns of perfectionism or nonassertiveness.
Belonging	Feelings of loneliness, intense longing for intimacy. Patterns of romanticism, codependency, sexual acting out.
Competence	Feelings of inadequacy, helplessness, failure, low self-esteem. Patterns of passivity or overcompensation.
Equity	Feelings of being vulnerable, victimized, and exploited; bitterness, anger, self-pity, and guilt. Patterns of power orientation, rigidity, defensiveness, giving up, or fatalism.
Identity	Feelings of confusion, emptiness, instability, falling apart. Difficulty making decisions, codependency, suppressed anger.
Security	Feelings of anxiety, mistrust, paranoia, uncertainty. Patterns of paranoia, compulsivity.
Significance	Feelings of worthlessness, low self-esteem, devaluation, jealousy, depression.
Transcendence	Feelings of meaninglessness, low spiritual well-being, anomie, boredom, hopelessness, chaos.

Fig. 4.1

EXPANSIVE EGO-DEFENSE MECHANISMS

Ego defenses are unconscious attempts to protect our ego from the anxiety and distress that arises when we are consciously aware of our failure to be perfect. They conspire to prevent us from facing the truth about ourselves. They promote self-deception. Ego defenses appear to be essentially automatic, although it is likely that those defenses used most frequently by a particular person are those that have been positively reinforced, that is, have been most effective in shielding a particular person from pain. This means that the highly defensive person not only lacks an accurate view of self and situations to make good choices but has less adaptive energy available to respond to stress in healthy ways.

The presence of ego defenses appears to be universal in post-Fall humanity. Their initial appearance biblically was full-blown and automatic in reaction to sin. Adam and Eve denied, blamed, rationalized, and displaced. The problem with ego defenses is that they prevent the person from gaining an accurate view of events. As a result, choices that might best address and manage stress may not be made. Instead, choices that amplify stress, especially in the long run, are likely to be made. The more ego defensiveness that is employed, the more psychic energy is bound up in maintaining the defenses.

Ego defenses that have not already been mentioned include repression, regression, isolation of effect, reaction formation, fixation, intellectualization, compensation, projection, fantasy, sublimation, identification, dissociation, and conversion reactions. A common expression of an ego defense is the *denial* that is used by alcoholics. This is often paired with displacement of hostility fueled by feelings of shame and failure.

> *Harold* constantly refused to admit that he had a drinking problem, or that he drank at all, in spite of a continuing pattern of long absences from the home for "walks" and half-empty bottles of alcohol hidden in different locations. When confronted with the evidence, he created incredible stories of how the bottles must have gotten there. If that did not work, he would become extremely hostile toward his wife and threaten violence.

He carried deep feelings of anger toward his father that had never been resolved. When he finally did act out his violence, hitting his wife in front of the children, she demanded that he get help or she and the children would leave.

Harold entered a Christian treatment program but immediately violated the rules by hiding cigarettes. He also projected his own hostility upon staff members, accusing them of being hostile and victimizing him. Needless to say, the treatment program did him little good, and he left before he was scheduled. Since that time Harold has lost his job and was finally kicked out of his home when he became physically abusive toward one of his children.

VAIN VALUES

Values are statements of what is most important in a person's life. Values act as organizers of one's resources. They are the structures and motivational foundation of our existence. They are also the standards by which we evaluate ourselves. They are, in effect, commitments to certain paths of life that appear as though they will ultimately grant us the most satisfaction and well-being. What is most valued receives the greatest share of our discretionary time, energy, effort, affection, and money. Values may be rated as to the degree of centrality that they occupy in our life.

Values interact with stress in at least two ways. First, anything that threatens our values generates substantial stress. They are defended more or less vigorously, depending on their centrality to our identity and commitments in life. Second, certain values may either increase or decrease the stress in a person's life. Vain values such as appearance, achievement, and affluence[10] may be culturally endorsed and promoted as the path to *shalom*. In truth, they increase stress because they are based on social comparison and bring only temporary relief from distress. Furthermore, pursuing these values may appear to meet certain ontological deficits while they are actually worsening others.

Stewart was a workaholic. His high achievements and productivity helped him to overcome deep feelings of loneliness because of the recognition and desirability those achievements gave to him. The intensity of his work commitments seemed to fill the deep emptiness that he felt inside, even though he was a Christian. In reality, however, commitment to achievement and affluence, as with his earlier involvement with athletic accomplishments (appearance), did not really touch his need to belong. Instead, it resulted in emotional separation from his wife. Ultimately, he chose the painful path of several affairs as apparent ways to find relief from the pain of his loneliness.

GENDER

As we have seen in chapter 3, the subjective experience or perception of events and social roles is largely shaped by socialization.[11] The influence of biological gender is also interpreted through psychosocial experience, as well as through genetic and hormonal channels. Gender is a fundamental component of personality.

Socialization into the female gender role, for example, prescribes that women be dependent, nonassertive, without control, and unselfishly responsive to the needs of others. Men are taught by instruction and example to keep their feelings locked inside. In Western society, men learn to be incessantly competitive.

It is generally believed that women suffer from greater psychological distress than men because the stressors in women's roles are more intense and persistent.[12] The developmentally shaped supportive and caretaking role of women in our society also means that women not only work primarily in helping professions but are more likely to be turned to as helpers in crisis situations.

Being male or female influences both the perception of a particular situation and the choice of coping responses to stress. With extraordinary consistency, women have been shown to be more likely than men to manifest depression and anxiety in response to stress. At the same time, they typically live longer with lesser and later incidence of heart disease. Men, in contrast, suffer less from anxiety and depression. However, they are at higher risk for heart disease at every age and have higher rates of premature death. Attempts to explain mortality differences in terms of employment-generated stress experience have failed because employment has actually improved women's health. Women are also more likely than men to hold stressful jobs. These are not necessarily high-level managerial positions, but jobs that are highly demanding and low in choice and control.

It is likely that the greater levels of psychological distress experienced by women (e.g. anxiety and depression) are due to more emotionally intense female roles. Women's roles require supportive responses to the needs of others as well as coping with their own stressful experiences. Women's social networks typically include a wider range of "others" and a deeper emotional involvement and concern for providing support even to the periphery of those networks. Women not only emotionally support husbands, children, other relatives, friends, and neighbors, but they are also likely to be involved in helping professions such as nursing, social work, and teaching.[13] Women are also more likely than men to be named as helpers in crisis situations. While involvement in these kinds of relationships provide some emotional benefits, the stressful consequences appear to be stronger than the beneficial ones.[14] The difference between the support a woman gives out and the emotional support she receives has been called the support gap.

Males and females seem to experience certain kinds of stress disorders with different frequency, are exposed to different types of stressors, attach different meanings to the same stressors, and cope with stress somewhat differently.[15] With regard to the kinds of stressors experienced, men are more likely to face the stresses of war and executive management. In addition to their pervasive supporter role, which we have discussed, women must cope with menstrual changes, pregnancy, the greater likelihood of physical or sexual assault, and the dual pressures of being both homemaker/caretaker and employee. While both men and women experience stress, more has been published on stress in the workplace and related to the male. As a result, we are focusing our attention more extensively on stress as related to women.

MOTHERHOOD

Unless a couple adopts, motherhood begins with pregnancy. This is one of the greatest changes in a woman's life and can be one of the most stressful times (especially the first pregnancy).

A related stress in a woman's life is the *in*ability to become pregnant. Disappointment from not conceiving causes considerable stress when pregnancy is desired. This, combined with expectations from family members and likely tension with her husband, can upset a woman's hormonal system, making it even less likely that she will get pregnant.

For the woman who does get pregnant, there are a host of probable physiological and emotional changes. These include morning sickness, pregnancy gingivitis, a kicking fetus, back pain,increased fatigue, sleeplessness, and changes in urination. In addition, the changes in her figure may negatively affect a woman's self-image, lead to stress-induced overeating, and interfere with sexual activity. She may also have to deal with toxemia and preeclampsia. Concerns over the wholeness and healthiness of the baby are uniquely hers as well as the impact of miscarriages and stillbirths.

Childbirth itself carries varying levels of increased stress for all women, as well. Additional stress may be experienced as the result of Cesarean sections. C-sections are major surgery and carry with them a death rate twice as high as normal vaginal delivery. Women who have the most social stressors and least emotional support, as measured by closeness with husband, family, and community, have significantly increased complications with both pregnancy and delivery.[16]

Finally, postpartum depression strikes some women. This may be the result of a combination of hormonal changes, new responsibility that is experienced as overwhelming, lack of childcare preparation, continuing interruption of sexual relations, and feelings of inadequacy.

Once the baby is born, a woman faces a new set of stressors in relation to parenting. Child-rearing is still seen as primarily the mother's responsibility, even in our egalitarian society. Each stage of motherhood has its unique stressors. The new mother is normally faced with increased responsibility, little help, and guilt over the tension between caregiving and personal desires such as a career or going back to school. Often she is more tired due to the nighttime needs of her infant, and she may feel less attractive.

Mothers also must contend with those on both ends of the spectrum who argue that they should devote themselves fully to either their career or to homemaking. Homemakers are criticized for not concentrating on reaching their full potential as adult women, while those pursuing a career are criticized for not giving enough of themselves to their children.

While the stress of dual-career mothering has been widely voiced, it is also important to recognize the stresses facing a full-time homemaker. In a world that measures a person's value by work production, housework holds low status. In addition, some of the factors that can increase the stress of a housewife are nonspecific time schedules, rewards that are not directly correlated to the quality of her work, dull and repetitive chores, and minimal time for relaxation and exercise. The wide range of responsibility requiring varied skills and dependence of several people upon her performance add stress, especially since she often has not had the specific training needed for her to feel competent.

The ability to prioritize roles, concentrate on one set of responsibilities at a time, and compromise standards are all important ingredients in her stress management.

STRESS IN THE WORKPLACE

Women are an increasing presence in the work force today, whether by necessity or choice. Stress on the job for the working woman is often experienced in getting less salary than men for doing similar work. Some jobs that are typically female-specific, such as waitressing and clerking, simply do not pay well. As a result, trying to make it financially is highly stressful if opportunities to improve one's job skills and to advance are not available. For single women, career advance is especially important. The resistance and resentment encountered from others is often a significant source of stress.

Harassment is another area of job-related stress that both single and married women face. The Supreme Court hearings involving Judge Clarence Thomas and Anita Hill brought an unprecedented focus upon sexual harassment. For a single woman this may be particularly stressful due to the lack of emotional support from a husband, which a married woman may have. For both single and married women, sexual harassment usually creates major stress because of the demeaning overtones and the threat of job demotion or loss if she does not comply.

For the single mother, the probabilities of significant stress are even greater than those of a married mother. Not only does she face the stress of trying to be both mother and father, but she most likely faces the struggles of inadequate income, insufficient time, the search for a caring baby-sitter, and the need for time to relax and time to socialize. Dating issues are a whole additional area of potential stress: how to even make time to date and how to make dating a positive experience for one's children are but two of the issues.

For the man who has internalized traditional standards of male competence in the workplace, the stress involved with trying to get ahead and to provide a high standard of living can be overwhelming. Psychogenic illness such as hypertension, gastrointestinal disorders, heart problems, asthma, and migraine headaches are part of the price many men pay to run in the corporate rat race. In addition, the demands of the job as interpreted by a high competitor typically increase stress by leading to the breakdown of marriage and family relations. Finally, many turn to drink, recreational drugs, or addictive television viewing for relief from the stress of the daily demands.

PREMENSTRUAL SYNDROME

Perhaps the most well-known expression of gender stress is that of PMS (premenstrual syndrome). For a great number of women, PMS is highly disruptive, generating or amplifying stress in their family, occupational, and interpersonal relationships.[17] There is also some evidence that PMS is antagonized by existing internal and external stress in a woman's life.

Up to 150 biological, psychological, and behavioral symptoms have been attributed to PMS.[18] Among these are depression, anxiety, anger, significant mood swings, irritability, headaches, nausea, palpitations, hot flashes, bloating, paranoia, sensitivity to rejection, suicidal ideation, insomnia, anorexia, food cravings, acne, decreased motivation, poor impulse control, and social isolation. As a result, some researchers argue that the designation really means nothing definitive. If it can be used to explain everything, it really does not explain anything.

Although there is considerable debate about definitive characteristics of PMS and scientific measurement, it appears that PMS is a crippling source of stress for a great number of women. It disrupts the lives of many women by placing intense stress on their family, job relationships/performance, and social relationships. Women suffering from PMS symptoms are not always quick to associate their symptoms with menstruation. Nevertheless, they may be consistently overwhelmed with apparently authentic self-defeating thoughts and behaviors that plunge them into feelings of self-doubt, anxiety about going crazy, and feelings of losing control at that time of the menstrual cycle.

COPING

Finally, there appear to be some basic differences in coping style that are gender-based. Women are more likely to use distraction and ignoring of stressful information. Men are more likely to deal with stress directly and aggressively. Women tend to display greater self-doubt and lower self-esteem than men. As children, boys are more optimistic about their performance and generalize less from past problems to new situations. Boys also are less likely to attribute failures to themselves (lack of intelligence, lack of ability, etc.).

SUMMARY

Human beings seem to automatically weave together a characteristic pattern of perceptions, ego defenses, emotions, values, and behaviors that are influenced by their gender. This integrative combination is called personality. These patterns of relating to one's self, to others, and to the world impact upon the experience of and response to stress that describes each person. Some personality orientations are more stress-dominated than others. There are also unique experiences of and responses to stress specifically associated with gender.

NOTES

1. Stella Chess, "Pathogenesis of the Adjustment Disorders: Vulnerabilities Due to Temperamental Factors," in *Stressors and the Adjustment Disorders*, ed. Joseph D. Noshpitz and R. Dean Coddington (New York: Wiley, 1990), 457–76.

2. Ibid., 461–63.

3. Ethel Roskies, *Stress Management for the Healthy Type A: Theory and Practice* (New York: Guilford, 1987).

4. Tina Adler, "Social Factors Link Hostility, Illness," *APA Monitor* (January 1991): 4–5.

5. See Craig W. Ellison, "Self-Esteem," in *Baker Encyclopedia of Psychology*, ed. David G. Benner (Grand Rapids: Baker, 1985), 1045–47.

6. Peter Freiberg, "Self-Esteem Gender Gap Widens in Adolescence," *APA Monitor* (April 1991): 29.

7. Ronald Potter-Efron and Patricia Potter-Efron, *Letting Go of Shame* (San Francisco: Harper and Row, 1989), 14.

8. Merle A. Fossum and Marilyn J. Mason, *Facing Shame: Families in Recovery* (New York: Norton, 1986).

9. I am grateful to James M. Harper and Margaret H. Hoopes, *Uncovering Shame: An Approach to Integrating Individuals and Their Family Systems* (New York: Norton, 1990) for their careful delineation of these characteristics of shame-producing families partially reflected here.

10. Craig W. Ellison, ed., *Your Better Self: Christianity, Psychology and Self-Esteem* (San Francisco: Harper and Row, 1983), 1–20.

11. I am particularly grateful for the research provided by Marcia Anderson, Leigh Flynn, Beth Mattsson-Boze, and Deborah Vassallo, "Stress in the Lives of Women," (project manuscript, Alliance Theological Seminary, December 1990). The portion of this chapter addressing gender relies heavily on their work.

12. Anderson et al., "Stress."

13. Deborah Belle, "Gender Differences in Social Moderators of Stress," in *Gender and Stress*, ed. R. C. Barnett, L. Biener, and G. K. Baruch (New York: The Free Press, 1987), 257–71.

14. Ibid., 258.

15. Dorothy H. G. Cotton, *Stress Management: An Integrated Approach to Therapy* (New York: Brunner-Mazel, 1990). For an even more expanded treatment see Barnett, Biener, and Baruch, *Gender and Stress*.

16. Donald R. Morse and M. Lawrence Furst, *Women Under Stress* (New York: Van Nostrand Reinhold, 1982).

17. Judith M. Abplanalp, "Psychosocial Theories," in *PMS: Premenstrual Syndrome*, ed. William R. Keye (Philadelphia: W. B. Saunders, 1988), 94–112.

18. I am especially indebted to Rebecca Eaton and Deborah Moon, "Uncovering the Truth and Myth about PMS," (project manuscript, Alliance Theological Seminary, December 1990).

Chapter Five

Twisted Thinking

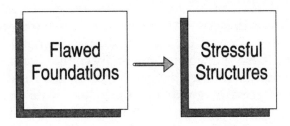

HUMAN BEINGS ARE MEANING-MAKERS. In order to survive we try to make sense out of experience. We not only *receive*, but we also *perceive*. That is, we constantly try to organize information into personally meaningful categories. These thought structures shape all of our subsequent interpretations, decisions, and behaviors.

The foundational meanings that we establish during early stages of development become structured as *controlling beliefs*. These mental structures filter subsequent experience and influence our views of everything. We hold to these beliefs because they help provide certainty and security. Some controlling beliefs are internalized as rules and act as psychomoral absolutes. Because these rules are learned in the context of our being evaluated as good or bad children, they have tremendous emotional force. They are resistant to change because the possibility of change, which requires violation of the inner rules, triggers strong emotional reactions (anxiety, fear, guilt). Violation of the rules in order to change them may threaten to overwhelm a person with feelings of being bad or despicable. Because thinking of ourselves in these shameful terms is very painful, there is a part of us (the False Self) that resists change. This is so even if the change would actually lead to less stress and pain in our lives in the long-run.

Controlling beliefs that promote distress may be grouped into two categories: **faulty filters** and **rotten rules.** *Faulty filters* are emotionally anchored beliefs about one's self, relationships, God, and life in general that are false. They serve as grids through which we interpret experience. For example, the belief that a person is the cause of his parents' horrible fights is a faulty filter. *Rotten rules* are the *shoulds* and *oughts, should nots* and *ought nots* that govern a person's choices in unhealthy and unholy ways. They are the internalized psychomoral rules that have either been spoken or nonverbally communicated by parents and other authority figures. To follow the rules is to feel that one is "good" (a good boy or girl); to violate them makes a person feel he or she is "bad." The rules act as an eleventh commandment. Children may not correctly perceive intended messages of parents and significant others, but the meanings they do perceive are internalized as absolutely true. Once internalized, these meanings act as controlling beliefs that govern their perception and behavior.

Both faulty filters and rotten rules are distortions. They do not tell the truth about reality as measured by God's view (given in the Bible) or as evaluated by a more objective third party, such as a therapist who is in tune with God's view. Even though these controlling beliefs may *feel* like they are absolutely true, they are false. They lock us into ways of perceiving and responding that contradict God's design for healthy living. In addition to giving a false picture of one's self, these distortions point people in wrong directions for meeting underlying psychospiritual needs. *They suggest ways to reduce stress that actually increase stress in the long run.*

Psychospiritual counseling maintains that Satan's battlefield is primarily in the minds and psyches of human beings. Because Satan hates God but has not been able to defeat him directly, he tries to establish his superiority by defeating and controlling human beings. He constantly seeks to dominate and devour us (see 1 Pet. 5:8) because we reflect God's image and (for Christians) possess the Holy Spirit.

There is a continual struggle between the False (fallen) and True (*imago Dei*) Self within each of us. Temptation includes the invitation to believe lies about ourselves, others, God, and reality and to mercilessly condemn ourselves for the wrongs that we have committed. If we yield to the temptation to believe Satan's lies, we discover that we experience psychospiritual, interpersonal, and spiritual fragmentation (see chapter 2).

Faulty Filters

Faulty filters deepen our ontological deficits. They feed us lies about our selves, God, and our world; present futile paths for overcoming our distress; and encourage self-condemnation and despair.[1] To the degree that we buy into these faulty filters, we build an inner reservoir of residual pain and stress. Often a particular filter will defensively shield us from the pain of one existential deficit only to open us to other pain because our twisted thinking prevents us from having a psychospiritual need met in a healthy way.

In this chapter we will examine a number of faulty filters as they relate to specific ontological deficits. This is not an exhaustive list, but it does highlight some of the most frequently encountered faulty filters. A specific faulty filter may cause or worsen different deficits in different people. Also, a specific filter may impact upon several ontological deficits in the same person. This is because it is unlikely that the eight givens/deficits are completely independent of each other.

We will look at several faulty filters and briefly describe case vignettes associated with each. Then we will comment briefly upon some of the most frequently expressed rotten rules.

Stress Intensifiers

First, we want to highlight several general stress intensifiers. These are controlling beliefs, not associated with specific deficits, that create a general psychospiritual climate of distress in those holding to them.

"God is against me." When Sylvia came for counseling she was severely depressed and felt sure that God did not intend for her to live for very long. The victim of steady verbal abuse from her father, who blamed her for everything including bad weather and business problems, Sylvia felt that God was against her too.

"Wait long enough and things will go wrong." Jason was fatalistic about life when he entered counseling. He was not especially down on himself, but he expected things to go wrong. He got tense when his life was going well. It was almost as though he sabotaged the good times in order to short-circuit the stress he felt because of uncertainty over when fate was going to lower the boom again.

"If you just try/work hard enough, things will be okay." Dan developed a pattern of intense workaholism, similar to that of his father and mother. Both parents were extremely active, rarely sat down to relax, and gave the message that the key to happiness was working hard enough. In reality, their busyness was a way to avoid vulnerability and more personal, emotionally based interaction. Dan's first wife left him because he was rarely at home and never took the time to talk with her or listen to her. He was unable to relax. Even on vacations he always had to be doing something or driving to get somewhere, so that his family ended vacations feeling exhausted.

"Life should be easier than it is." Phyllis and her family had been in therapy for approximately ten years when she came to see me. It quickly became evident that the family had a tendency to think that every problem they faced was unusual and too difficult to handle. They literally made mountains out of molehills and were convinced that they could not handle such difficulties on their own. Part of the counseling process involved helping them to see that every person and family faces problems and crises and that life is not easy but can be coped with without leaning on a therapist.

ACCEPTANCE/REJECTION

Faulty filters that promote the feeling of rejection somehow communicate to the person that he or she is bad, guilty, undesirable, shameful, or not good enough. Although the filters of rejection are built by others, a person's major struggle as an adult may be with feelings of self-doubt and self-rejection.

"Who I am is not okay." Rhonda believed that the very essence of her being was ugly and despicable. Her mother seemed to constantly communicate the wish that Rhonda were someone else. Rhonda knew that she had been born during a very difficult time in her mother's life and felt that she was not wanted. Although her mother did not openly blame her, she felt as though her parents' marital difficulties and her mother's nervous breakdown (when Rhonda was small) were all her fault. She felt that she was a reminder of her mother's imperfection and being out of control at that time in her life. As a result, she was constantly critical of herself, was always striving to achieve something greater (another degree, a better job), and was constantly tense.

"There is something different/strange/weird about me." Marsha felt that her family always regarded her as strange and patronized her. As a result, she became something of an actress, trying to be for them and for everyone else the kind of person that others would like. She came in for counseling when she realized that she really did not know who the real Marsha was.

Calvin remembers his mother actually commenting there was "something different" about him when he was four years old. It was said in a way that he understood was not affirming. One of his intense fears when he came for counseling was that he might be gay, even though he was not attracted to men and had never even experimented sexually with another male.

"I'm bad. I make life miserable for people because I upset them." Charlene's mother constantly complained about the stress she was under because of Charlene. She never hugged Charlene or told her that she loved her. Instead, she pointed out countless imperfections she saw in Charlene.

BELONGING/LONELINESS

Faulty filters that establish the deficit of loneliness in a person set a person up to believe that he or she is not wanted, and is not worth being with or truly known, is undesireable, unattractive, unable to make friendships, weird, or different from others.

"If people really knew me, they wouldn't like me." Ruth Anne realized that whenever friendships began to get close, she would back away emotionally. She was an attractive young woman and had even gotten as far as being engaged on two occasions, but she had ended the relationships shortly after engagement. In counseling we discovered that she withdrew because she was convinced that people would reject her if they really knew what she was like. Her mother had repeatedly said, "If people only knew you like I do . . ." in the context of disapproval of her actions. This promoted both a self-perception of badness and an emotional and social isolation due to significant self-doubt.

"I'm not lovable, and I can't give love." Rosalind's mother must have been a marine disciplined for unnecessary roughness. I began to understand the roots of Rosalind's difficulties with self-esteem and intimacy when the three of us met for counseling. Her mother was just plain harsh. She seemed to carry a blazing verbal machine-gun with her. Even though Rosalind had become a passive person who had spent much of her twenty-seven years trying to please her mother, she had never succeeded. She had considerable anger toward men (reflective of her mother's negative attitudes toward her ex-husband, Rosalind's father). She was troubled by a deep sense of rage and self-doubt that flared up whenever she felt someone was not listening to her or was treating her as though she did not count.

"No one really wants me." Estella's father walked out on her mother when she was five years old. He died of a drug overdose about a year later. Her mother left Estella with her grandmother most of the time, while she worked and partied. Estella's grandmother openly complained that it was just too much for her to take care of Estella and her two brothers.

When Estella was ten, she was sent to live with an aunt and uncle who seemed very uninterested in her, except for demanding that she cook meals and take care of the housecleaning. Estella finally ran away from them when she was thirteen, but was returned when no foster home placements were found. She became promiscuous as a teen, finding comfort in being held close, but began to realize that men only wanted her body.

By the time she was twenty-two she had tried to commit suicide twice.

COMPETENCE/INADEQUACY

Faulty filters that encourage the deficit of inadequacy are beliefs that one is incompetent, unable to perform at an acceptable level, stupid, a klutz, a loser, or otherwise inferior to others and unable to handle the basic tasks of life in a satisfactory manner.

"I can't do anything right." Greg was extremely reluctant to try anything new. Even though his wife got angry at him for not doing anything around the house, he felt totally incapable. On the rare occasions when he did try to fix something, he gave up before long, calling himself "stupid," "imbecile," and other demeaning names. He had taken a maintenance job because he did not feel he could do anything else without making mistakes. As a result, he was under constant financial stress. When growing up, Greg remembers his father being extremely impatient and ripping tools out of his hands because he was doing things the wrong way or too slowly. His mother would always emphasize the mistakes on the papers he brought home from school.

"Life is too much for me; I can't take it." Eva feels overwhelmed by life. As a child, her mother helped Eva to do almost everything and discouraged her from doing things on her own. She was rarely allowed to go to friends' homes in the neighborhood to play. She was home-schooled due to her parents' concerns about humanistic philosophy and about her safety in the public school. Her parents rarely expressed a sense of confidence in her but seemed to feel that she needed to be helped and protected, even as a thirty-year-old adult still living with them.

"I don't need help; I can handle everything by myself." Michael works incredibly long hours as a minister. He feels that because he is getting paid to minister he should handle the bulk of the church responsibilities by himself. He is also a bit perfectionistic and does not feel that he can trust others to do things as well as he can. The toll has been rising, however, as he recently has begun to feel irritable, isolated, and burned out.

EQUITY (MORALITY)/VICTIMIZATION

The faulty filters of victimization and inequity are constructed on the belief that one is a victim, treated unfairly, exploited and manipulated by others, the object of unjust scorn or discrimination, unable to do anything actively to control one's life experience, or required to do more than is fair to get through life, or that God (the gods) are against one.

"People always take advantage of me, and I can't stop them." Stephen was the youngest of five sons. Throughout childhood he was picked on by his brothers, had money stolen and toys broken by them, and was blamed for things he did not do. In school his peers treated him the same way. Gradually he became withdrawn and fatalistic, without any goals or direction in life. In his early twenties he began drinking and was only able to hold temporary jobs. He felt that life was one big ripoff.

"I don't have any right to my own wishes; everything has to be what my mother wants." Chelsea's mother was highly domineering and verbally abusive. Her father was passive and acquiescent to her mother's demands. The only person who seemed to have needs that were considered important was her mother. Chelsea's needs were ignored or discounted and devalued. In fact, it was only after being threatened by a school social worker that her mother finally took Chelsea to the dentist to get several decayed teeth fixed.

"I don't have any power to change things." Mickey's parents did not listen to him because they were too busy arguing. Even though he tried to find ways to get them to stop fighting and his father to quit drinking, nothing seemed to work. Mickey finally concluded that he had no control over events in his life.

"I can't count on people or God to be there when I need them." Alicia had been hospitalized for a serious illness when she was two years old. Her single mother did not visit her during the five days she was there because she was too busy. When Alicia had her first child, her husband failed to come to the hospital because he had planned an evening out with some friends and did not want to spoil it. When her grandmother became ill and she prayed intensely that God would spare this woman who had shown her love, she died. Alicia felt as though she was a

victim of life, abandoned and alone, not worth enough for anyone to care about.

"I feel that God made a mistake with me. Why did he let me be born?" Tina felt that she had let everybody down by her drinking, drug use, dropping out of school, and turning to prostitution. She did not understand herself but felt tremendously guilty for even existing.

Identity/Confusion

Faulty filters involving identity confusion establish self-perceptions of self-doubt, uncertainty about correct boundaries and selfishness, questioning of one's purpose in life, gender confusion, and apprehension about having a unique sense of individuality.

"I can't trust myself." Paul was constantly blamed by his parents when he made mistakes. They told him that he should always check with them before making decisions or trying new things because they had more experience. By the time he was a teenager he was plagued with considerable self-doubt.

"I am nothing." Sheila had been emotionally abused from early childhood. She remembers her father telling her numerous times that if it were not for him she would not exist. Her mother was domineering and controlling. Sheila felt as though she was not supposed to have any thoughts or feelings of her own but was expected to look at things the way her mother did. On the few occasions when she had tried to express her own differing viewpoints, her mother acted either angry or hurt.

"I'll never amount to a pile of rubbish." Matt will never forget the day when his alcoholic father, who was barely able to hold occasional menial jobs, yelled at him, "You'll never amount to a pile of rubbish!" He has spent most of his adult life trying to disprove that statement by becoming a success. His drive to be a success (he had become a very wealthy professional) had largely fractured his marriage and family when he decided he needed help because everything was falling apart and he felt like a failure.

"I am bad; I deserve punishment." Brendan's physically abusive parents told him he was bad and deserved punishment as they battered him for whatever they considered an infraction. During the course of childhood, he internalized this belief and thought of himself as a terrible person.

Sarah felt exactly the same due to sex play that she had engaged in with neighborhood boys at the initial invitation of her brother when she was eight years old. She had been unable to shake the feelings of shame and need for punishment. Although married, she was sexually frigid and emotionally withdrawn much of the time.

"I exist to make men (sexually) happy." Anne was a strikingly beautiful woman who was scarred by her self-identity. The victim of sexual abuse by her grandfather at age five, her uncle at age seven, her older brother when she was eight, and ultimately her stepfather from age eleven to fourteen, she felt that her only reason for being was to be sexual and make men happy. She was, in fact, tremendously depressed. She had been promiscuous throughout her teen years and had gotten heavily into drugs for a period of a year and a half before realizing she was destroying herself.

"I'm a nonperson unless I'm a sweet little caretaker." Corine was an extremely sweet woman who came for counseling in a confused and depressed mood. She had spent her whole life trying to make her family happy, to no avail. She had been married for six years and tried to do everything she could to help her husband. He was staying out "working" until midnight every night, was nasty to her when he was around, and refused to give her money to take care of her basic needs and the baby in spite of his eighty-five-hour "work" week. Corine felt she was helpless and was ready to fall apart because all of her caretaking had never worked.

Security/Anxiety

The faulty filters that promote the ontological deficit of anxiety are fear-based. They stress vulnerability, danger, external locus of control, possible failure, and possible condemnation. The mind-set is one of catastrophizing or believing that bad things are likely to occur.

"Life is dangerous." After a life-threatening illness as an infant, Brent's grandmother communicated this message to him by being solicitous and overprotective. At the same time, his father verbally and nonverbally communicated a message that he was weak and not tough enough. And yet the only time his father

seemed to pay any attention was when Brent was sick. As a result, as an adult Brent got highly anxious over any signs of illness or pain. He found it difficult to persevere in any work or inter-personal situations that made demands on him. He bad-mouthed his wife for not caring about him when she did not give him all the grandmotherly nurturing that he wanted when he was sick.

"God will destroy me if I don't do things right." Larry was ex-tremely anxious and stress-filled, highly obsessive, and com-pulsive as a result of this belief. He spent hours each day reading the Bible and praying. He was obsessed with doing everything the way God wanted him to. He was deathly afraid that God was going to send him to hell.

"I might have committed the unpardonable sin." Typically, this belief is associated with a sense of deep shame due either to parental messages of rejection or behaviors that violated moral standards. Henry was paralyzed in anxiety over this due to some sexual exploration that he had engaged in with his younger sister when he was ten and she was seven years old. Even though he had subsequently acted in a scrupulously moral way with women and was still a virgin at age twenty-nine, he was plagued by this thought. He even had to be hospitalized for three months. Not coincidentally, his parents had perfectionistic moral, academic, and occupational stan-dards. He was still living with them when he began counseling.

"Life is out of my control; bad things might happen to me if I venture too far from home or ride in elevators." Esther was agoraphobic. She found it almost impossible to ride in an elevator, drive over major bridges, or go on trips. As a girl she had tuberculosis, and several members of her family had died from it. She had one lung removed during her thirties. She was extremely afraid of being helplessly stranded in any place where she might not be able to get competent medical help. At the same time that she felt life was out of her control, she was very controlling of her adult daughter and husband.

SIGNIFICANCE/WORTHLESSNESS

The deficit of worthlessness is established by faulty filters that emphasize that a person is of little value, replaceable, not missed when absent, unwanted, or not worth spending time or energy with. They convey the message that a person is devalued and a nobody.

"I've always felt like I wasn't valued; nobody ever asked me what I thought about things." In Roy's home, children were supposed to be seen and not heard. They were supposed to be compliant and obedient. Both of Roy's parents worked and spent considerable time socializing with other adult friends in their free time. They always seemed to humor him as the youngest while at least occasionally paying attention to what his older sister and brother had to say. Consequently he was rather introverted, which resulted in his teachers ignoring him as well.

"I don't think that anybody really cares whether I'm dead or alive." Ted's father never spent any time with him, except to yell at him for something he had forgotten to do. A poor student in school, Ted was a loner with only one good friend, who moved away when he was in tenth grade. He got a job doing cleaning for a large company at nights after high school. He has worked there as a janitor for the past twelve years. Ted was always too shy to date and lived alone. His parents almost never initiated contact with him to see how he was doing. Ted was referred for counseling after he had slit his wrists in a suicide attempt.

"Once I get enough money, people will notice me and think I'm somebody." Geoff was the youngest of seven children. By the time he came along, his parents were exhausted just trying to keep up with the activities and needs of his older brothers and sisters. He became the missing person in the family—silent and withdrawn. He felt as though he was not important or worth noticing to his family. Geoff often overheard his parents talking about their difficult financial situation and made up his mind when he was twelve that he was going to be rich. That way people (and his parents in particular) would notice him and consider him valuable.

TRANSCENDENCE/MEANINGLESSNESS AND SPIRITUAL ISOLATION

Faulty filters of meaninglessness and spiritual isolation entrench such controlling beliefs as there is no purpose beyond the here and now, God does not exist or is uninvolved in human affairs, a relationship with God is not possible or desirable, or life is just a farce and death is meaningless.

"I don't seem to have any direction in life." Mark was depressed and confused when he entered counseling. Since high school he had spent eighteen years of his life wandering from location to location, from job to job. Nothing seemed to motivate him. As he approached forty he realized that he was aimless and that his life was slipping by him in a meaningless way. The one person who had motivated him several years ago, a woman whom he loved greatly, had rejected him. He still carried that wound along with a sense of hopelessness. Although he had been raised as a Catholic and had maintained an interest in religious things, he had never made a clear commitment to God and had not been able to put his life into the framework of a larger purpose.

"My life seems so empty; isn't there any more to life?" It hit Don one Thursday night as he sat in front of the television: Day after day it was the same routine—up at 6 A.M., dress and take the train to work, work from 8:30–5:00, take the train home, eat supper, collapse in front of the television for two hours, and go to bed. He had followed this schedule for the past twenty years. Only one child, a teenager who wanted to live his own independent life, remained at home. He was bored with Doris, his wife, as well. They had little in common and rarely talked, played, or made love together.

Rotten Rules

Rotten rules are similar to faulty filters except that they carry with them the sense of being commandments. They govern a person's choices, feelings, and behaviors by providing a structure of *shoulds* and *oughts*. They tell a person how to live life so there is minimal (apparent) pain and how to meet psychospiritual needs.

The issue is not that they are rules. Human beings in societies seem to *need* rules to guide their functioning. The problem is that rotten psychomoral rules are not biblically warranted. (See figure 5.1 for a list of some of the most frequent rotten rules.) They are usually antagonistic to a balanced reading of Scripture and a healthy experience of life. They imprison people because they *feel* like they are right. Any attempt to alter rotten

Rotten Rules

Thou shalt make others happy at all times.

Thou shalt not be satisfied with thy self.

Thou shalt not express thy feelings.

Thou shalt not make commitments.

Thou shalt never be good enough; thou shalt never
  amount to anything.

Thou shalt be a caretaker of anyone who has needs.

Thou shalt be happy.

Thou shalt be irresponsible.

Thou shalt be overly responsible.

Thou shalt not make waves or rock the boat.

Thou shalt be loyal to thy parents and family.

Thou shalt be incompetent and helpless.

Thou shalt not trust thyself.

Thou shalt not let people get close to thee.

Fig. 5.1

rules initially triggers feelings of terrible badness (shame),
anxiety, disloyalty, and other imprisoning emotions. Normally,
a person has to be willing to tolerate these frightening emotions and condemning thoughts with the gentle support of a
counselor while consciously choosing to break the rules in order to gain relief and construct a balanced and healthy set of
rules that promote *shalom*.

ACCEPTANCE/REJECTION

Rotten rules that focus on avoidance of rejection establish
unrealistic, unhealthy, and conditional terms for being able to
feel accepted and acceptable.

"Avoid pain at all costs—it will destroy you." Cathy was raised in an abusive home environment where she was verbally run down by her father and spanked excessively until she was about fourteen. Her father also occasionally locked her in a closet for punishment. Her mother communicated rotten rules such as "Don't have dreams," "Don't make plans," and "You'll fail." In order to avoid the pain of this kind of treatment, Cathy became extremely nonassertive. She found it initially difficult to take the risks necessary to overcome her passivity.

"Be perfect (so you will be acceptable)." Andrea felt that she was a terrible mother and a poor wife. She frequently felt she was unacceptable, no good, and ashamed, although she was attractive. Her husband clearly loved her and was not critical of her. As we explored the roots of her struggles, we discovered that Andrea firmly believed that she had been a mistake. She felt that she had to buy acceptance from her mother by being good enough. Both her mother and her sister treated her as though she was incompetent, so Andrea was highly self-critical and dissatisfied with her own attempts at parenting. She was afraid that she would not do it exactly right and would be blamed by her mother for not being good enough.

"Don't do anything that would upset people." Claudia got the message that she was responsible for making her parents happy. Her father was a negative person who always complained about things. Her mother had shared her unhappiness about their relationship and about her unhappy childhood with Claudia. As a result, Claudia felt that it was her responsibility to take care of and emotionally protect her fragile mother. She felt that she had to keep everything on an emotional even keel in the home. She began to struggle with depression and resentment toward her parents in her twenties, but she continued to be a caretaker with them and in other relationships. The needs of others always came before her own, and she found it difficult to share her own feelings with others.

BELONGING/ISOLATION

Rotten rules that provide unsatisfactory paths for dealing with the stress and pain of possible isolation emphasize *avoiding* the pain of loneliness through mistrust, performance, people pleasing, and perfectionism, which are strategies that *prevent intimacy* rather than encourage it.

"Don't get too close to others or you'll get hurt." Other versions of this distortion are, "People always have a hidden agenda," and "Don't trust." Bruce's parents were both alcoholics, though he did not fully understand this until he was in his late teens. They would rip him apart verbally when they were drunk, which was at least three times a week. Even though he got himself up in the morning, made his own meals, had a job at a local deli after school, and managed to keep his grades at a B level, they constantly criticized him for being irresponsible and a burden to them. When he was sixteen he got emotionally involved with Suzanne and shared his heart with her, only to have her drop him after about six months and tell others the secrets he had shared with her. From that point on, Bruce found it virtually impossible to initiate friendships or to reveal anything about his real thoughts and feelings.

"Be a success or superstar—everyone will like you." Clarence was an impeccably dressed man in his early thirties who had obviously made it. He drove a Mercedes, had a condominium by a lake, and was nationally rated as the number two person in sales in his company. He was also desperately lonely. He had had a number of relationships after his wife divorced him in his late twenties because he was married to his career. The relationships were temporary, heavily sexualized, and left him feeling empty. He had begun drinking and came in for counseling when he realized he was starting to lose control. People indeed wanted to be associated with him as a top star, but he also sensed that they were not really interested in him as a person; rather they were trying to attach themselves to him in order to advance their careers (just as he had done).

"Make people happy (so they'll want to be your friends)." Corey had always been the resident clown. He discovered that he could make his parents pay attention to him by being funny and that he could do the same thing with peers in school. As an adult in the work world, he polished his comedic abilities. People loved to be around him, waiting for the next witticism or joke. Gradually, however, Corey began to have an uneasy feeling that grew into severe anxiety as he wondered if people would

like him if he were not a comedian. He began to realize that he was, in fact, very much alone, because he had avoided close relationships for fear that the real (noncomedic) Corey would not be wanted.

"I must be unconditionally loved." Heidi was on her third marriage and not feeling very good about it. She felt that Ralph did not fully appreciate her and was critical of her, just like her previous two husbands had been. In each case, when the husbands began to express differences of opinion and did not spend all of their free time with her, she began to feel unloved. She seemed to overlook a variety of other expressions of love by Ralph and focused on anything he said that could be interpreted as nonloving.

EQUITY/VICTIMIZATION

Rotten rules that govern those struggling with victimization set people up to be passive and to allow others to take advantage of them.

"Don't be selfish; you shouldn't hang onto personal rights." Sally's parents communicated this rule to her by interpreting any activity, desire, or event that she wanted as selfish. They taught her that she was a very selfish person who should make sure that other people's wishes were met regardless of the cost to her. She learned that she was a bad person if she had any wishes or beliefs of her own and that she existed to serve others.

IDENTITY/IDENTITY CONFUSION

Rotten rules governing identity confusion establish any sense of self as separate or self as having dreams and synthesizing goals to be bad or selfish.

"Don't be selfish." This can be appropriate advice. Sometimes, however, it is actually a crippling, dysfunctional parental rule that conveys the message that the child does not have a right to an independent sense of self. This is often the case in codependency. Marilyn, for example, grew up feeling she had no right to establish self-boundaries of preferences, desires, beliefs, and behaviors that distinguished her from her mother. Her mother constantly met any signs of separate identity in Marilyn with anger about her rebellion or selfishness, or with

tears and complaints about how all Marilyn cared about was herself. In the latter outbursts, she would accuse Marilyn of not truly loving her.

SECURITY/ANXIETY

Rotten rules that establish the stress of anxiety literally command people to worry, to try and control everything lest something bad happens, to protect themselves, and to believe that others have malicious motives, that they are not strong or competent enough to take care of themselves, or that it is not right for them to take care of themselves.

"Be vigilant—watch out for danger." Tom, Roger and Skip were raised in a home where they experienced serious physical and emotional abuse from their father. As a result of their vulnerability and helplessness in the face of unpredictable and uncontrolled rage, they each developed severe anxiety disorders as adults. Whenever they experienced the feelings of being taken advantage of, loss of control, or continued expressions of anger from their father, they suffered anxiety attacks as their bodies and emotions unsuccessfully sought to defend against apparent danger. Tom developed a pattern of severe anxiety about illness, which led to many days taken off from work (he worked with his father) and tension with his wife over his being home and the financial implications of lost work time. Roger also developed panic attacks triggered in part by the internalization of anger toward Tom because of the extra load Roger had to carry when Tom was "sick" (he also worked for his father). Roger was a people pleaser who continued to struggle with his frequently bombastic father. Skip developed a serious anxiety disorder that was fed by deep self-doubt as a result of the verbal/emotional abuse and high levels of coercive control he had experienced while growing up. This had nearly incapacitated him when he entered counseling with an obsessive focus on swallowing.

SIGNIFICANCE/WORTHLESSNESS

Rotten rules that trap people in the deep deficit of worthlessness command them to be humble (to not think well of themselves), tell them they will never make it, or command them to be world-class superstars (usually not attainable or attainable only by living a life of extraordinary self-criticism and stress).

"Be perfect." Tom learned that the only way to get any attention from his parents was to be an academic and athletic superachiever. Even when he brought home straight A's in high school and was named to the all-state track team, his accomplishments were met by the equivalent of a yawn: "That's nice; now, it's time for you to do the lawn. And remember that you need to clean your room better; you left it in a mess this morning. By the way, what about the job you were going to get to help us out a bit?"

NOTES

1. For an expanded treatment of a variety of such distortions, see Chris Thurman, *The Lies We Believe* (Nashville: Thomas Nelson, 1989).

Chapter Six

The Pressure Cooker

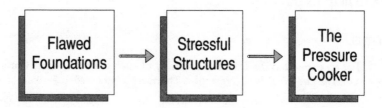

THE SIZE OF AN INDIVIDUAL'S STRESS RESERVOIR and the amount of residual stress within that reservoir as a person reaches adulthood are the result of flawed foundations and stressful structures. If a person's thinking and emotional processes are distorted, he or she will have a bigger gateway through which new stressors may enter. People who have experienced significant levels of stress during childhood will more easily overflow with stress when day-to-day current stressors are added. Stress becomes more intense and faster and is experienced more frequently for adults with distorted structures and large amounts of residual stress.

Current sources of stress that may impact an adult include biological, environmental, institutional, psychosocial, and spiritual stressors (see figure 6.1).

BIOLOGICAL STRESSORS

People are stressed by such biological events as accidents, birth-related trauma, bodily trauma (assault, battery, rape),

Current Stressors

Biological

aging process
allergies
hormonal changes/
   imbalances
illness
lack of adequate sleep
disrupted biorythms
seasonal affective disorder
stimulus overload
xanthine stimulants

Environmental

natural disasters
human-assisted disruptions
   of environment
uncontrollable noise
crowding

Spiritual

demonization
temptation
trials/suffering for faith

Psychosocial

abuse
addictions
codependency
devaluation/rejection
death of loved one
divorce
unresolved conflict
unrealistic expectations (of self
   or others)
unfavorable comparison with
   others
perfectionism
inadequate communication and
   intimacy skills
poor time management skills

Institutional

Adverse workplace conditions
   and demands
economic instability and
   poverty
war
prejudice
dehumanizing governmental or
   organizational policies

Fig. 6.1

acute illness, chronic illness, genetic abnormalities, hormonal imbalances, premenstrual syndrome, puberty-based changes, surgical traumas, and toxic ingestions. These stressors not only affect the person suffering from them, but frequently they create significant stress upon other family members.

*As the result of a tragic football injury, **Brian** became a quadriplegic. Formerly an athletic and energetic person, he was confined to a wheelchair, unable to move except for his head. The girl he was engaged to marry was supportive initially but eventually broke their engagement. Brian is now totally dependent upon others for every aspect of his daily life. His plans to complete the senior year of college have been placed on hold indefinitely. In the two years since his accident, Brian has alternated between fits of anger and pits of depression, wishing that God had let him die instead of leaving him as a vegetable. The financial costs of his hospitalization and care have been astronomical. These costs, together with the demands of his daily care are taking a major toll on his mother and father as well. There seems to be no way out of the stress.*

ENVIRONMENTAL STRESSORS

Environmental stressors may be divided into physical and institutional groups. Those that are *natural disasters* include earthquakes, hurricanes, floods, tornadoes, and blizzards. *Human-assisted environmental stressors* also involve the environment but are somehow affected by human decision-making or neglect. Such stressors include radioactivity (e.g., Chernobyl and Three Mile Island), toxic contamination (e.g., Love Canal, New York), global warming, ozone depletion, and the possibilities of a nuclear or petroleum winter (e.g., destructive burning of oil refineries and supplies in the Persian Gulf).

The daily stressors of uncontrollable noise, crowding, and air pollution that millions of urban residents face create significant stress. For example, breathing the air in major cities such as New York is equivalent to smoking almost two packs of cigarettes per day![1] Pollution triggers stress through its negative demands upon both physical and emotional adaptation. It costs about six billion dollars per year to treat pollution-generated respiratory diseases, according to the United States Public Health Service. Burning eyes, headaches, dizziness, and sinus problems lower one's life quality and increase stress. Higher levels of air pollution have been found to be associated with both psychiatric emergencies,[2] and higher psychiatric hospital admissions.[3] Subjection to nontoxic but unpleasant air has been shown to increase fatigue, aggression, and anxiety, while decreasing ability to concentrate.[4] Over three million children (one out of six) have levels of lead high enough to cause significant neurological impairment; over 67 percent of black inner-city children have been contaminated.[5]

There is new evidence that a high-frequency, barely detectable squeal coming from the back of most computer terminals causes stress, especially in women. Such stress-induced reactions as anxiety, irritability, headaches, fatigue, and nausea are reported as potentially linked to the computer squeal.[6] There is even some concern that miscarriages may be linked to video display terminal users.

INSTITUTIONAL STRESSORS

Workplace conditions and demands that do not take human physical or psychological needs into account cause institutional stressors. These include such things as shifts that rotate weekly, as is often the case with police or nursing personnel. Normal biorhythms are significantly disrupted, sleep is disturbed, and the ability to maintain normal interpersonal relationships impaired by such a pattern. Also, demands that do not allow for worker decision-making and that continually stretch a person to the limit to try to meet production quotas, report deadlines, system transitions, and profit-making goals of the company create substantial stress. This is eventually expressed in lower quality of work, illness, and absenteeism. It also results in negative interpersonal and familial fallout.

Power-oriented management practices, which leave employees feeling depersonalized and exploited, as well as the encouragement of colleague competitiveness (one has to climb to the top on the backs of coworkers), which increases levels of mistrust and interpersonal isolation, are significant institutional stressors. "Injuries leading to compensation and time off, and mental disorders resulting from job experiences have multiplied so drastically in the last decade that gradual mental stress claims exceed those filed for other occupational diseases. In California alone, stress-related claims increased by almost 450 percent between 1982–1986."[7]

Due to a combination of work demands, economic conditions, and an increasingly strong desire on the part of Americans to have it all, many Americans find themselves on a treadmill of ambition (some call it greed). This leaves little time for relaxation or meaningful relationships with friends, spouses, or children. The amount of leisure time that the average American enjoys has shrunk by 37 percent between 1973–1989, while the average work week has increased from forty-one to forty-seven hours, and the two-income family has become the norm. Researchers indicate that addiction to an accelerated schedule leads to the typical stress-induced physical breakdowns, difficulty relaxing when there is time, children taking care of children in the absence of parents, and other emotional and relational difficulties.[8]

Martin and Ruth were having serious marital conflict due largely to the lack of marital and familial interaction by Martin, who was being pressed to produce more and more in the face of announced company layoffs. He felt he had to work six and a half days a week to do his job, and typically he would be gone from 7 A.M. to 8 P.M. Ruth felt totally abandoned, and the children kept asking for Martin to stay home and play with them.

The stresses of war, poverty, institutional prejudice, threatened terrorism, and failing savings and loan institutions and banks are additional institutional stressors. Incredible stress has been generated as the result of economic, political, and housing policies that have left millions out of work or with grossly inadequate incomes and the multiplied stresses of homelessness. On the sidewalk under the Manhattan Bridge in New York City are several homeless people living in cardboard boxes. As I talked with two of the men late one night, I learned that over half of them had regular jobs but could not afford to pay exorbitant housing costs and taxes and still eat. This is the case for thousands in our cities. Others in both urban and rural areas are barely getting by with low-level incomes. They live under the daily stress of hoping that nothing goes wrong, because they have no extra money for medical bills, house repairs, or emergencies.

PSYCHOSOCIAL STRESSORS

Psychosocial stressors include:

negativism	passivity (nonassertiveness)
codependency	phobias
disillusionment with others	parenting
inadequate relational/ intimacy skills	unfavorable comparisons with others
unresolved conflicts	sexual dysfunctions
blaming of or by others	stress-enhancing values
poor time management	physical or emotional abuse
devaluation/rejection	perfectionism
irresponsible or over- responsible behavior patterns	unrealistic expectations of others or of one's self

These stressors can also include a variety of addictive, neurotic, and psychotic conditions that may be triggers, amplifiers, or faulty coping responses to stress.

Death and divorce are two especially potent sources of psychosocial stress. Human beings are fundamentally relational beings who form interpersonal attachments, which in turn shape their very sense of identity. A parent's death is especially traumatic for children. The suffering and death of children or the unexpected death of a spouse who is not elderly is highly stressful for adults. The loss of several loved ones in a short period of time, or together in an accident or war tragedy, is traumatic as well. The impact of loss through death depends, of course, upon the degree of bonding, the availability of other intimate support, and the general emotional health of the one bereaved.

Divorce is more stressful for a longer period of time than was once thought to be the case.[9] The impact of divorce is probably the greatest on younger children,[10] but it is also significant for older children and the spouse who perceives himself or herself as victim. One of the surprising findings of Wallerstein's study is that even those who *initiate* divorce struggle with stress for substantial periods of time.

Finally, stimulus overload and overchoice cause significant stress in the lives of many urban Americans. The average urban dweller or worker is confronted daily with a mass of stimuli. Every stimulus that is experienced needs to be processed (automatically screen out, choose to ignore, screen for implications, explore, defend against, or interact). The result is heightened stress.

This is compounded further by the media-generated norm that we **need** to be highly informed. We try to keep up with what is happening throughout our community, profession, nation, and world each day through newspapers, radio, professional newsletters, computer services, and television. Because there are so many choices of what to do with the little leisure time that we have, many people find it difficult to make decisions because they are afraid they will miss out on something. "Have you seen . . . ?" or "Have you read . . . ?" questions from others become sources of stress and feelings of inadequacy for many.

SPIRITUAL STRESSORS

Spiritual stressors are based on the assumption that there is a real spiritual domain that is able to interact with human beings. Throughout Christian history three spiritually based sources of stress have been recognized. These are:

- temptations—the invitation and impulse to choose contrary to God's laws for living;
- trials—some form of suffering or persecution related to one's faith commitment;
- demonization—attempts by satanic forces to influence and control the choices and lives of people.

I have not included persistent turmoil over whether one is truly saved or has committed the unpardonable sin under this category of stressors. Those issues are normally best understood as a reflection of psychosocial or biological dysfunction (e.g., obsessive-compulsive disorder) with religious ideation. However, it is still wise to at least consider the possibility of a spiritually generated disorder.

CLUSTER STRESS

Although we have tried to distinguish between classes of stressors, it should be obvious that such distinctions are somewhat arbitrary. Many environmental events have social overtones. Most stressors are at least partially psychological in that their impact depends upon the psychological hardiness and the perceptions of the person exposed to them. Frequently, several stressors within a category and several categories of stressors may be pushing themselves upon a person at the same time. The combination and interaction of stressors can be expected both to intensify and complicate the process of counseling intervention.

An example of cluster stress involving the interaction of residual and current stressors is Louise.[11]

> **Louise** is the fifth of nine children. She is now in her forties. Both of her parents were heavy drinkers. Her mother was both emotionally and physically abusive. On one occasion she threw boiling water at Louise's face; on another she threw a knife at her sister. Louise's mother read palms and tea leaves and used the ouija board. No matter what Louise did, she could not win her mother's approval. Her role was to be the family servant, and her mother made her the primary object of her constant wrath. Louise's older brother sexually molested her as well.
>
> When Louise was fifteen she got pregnant by a drug addict, whom she married. The marriage lasted about three years and was a nightmare of abuse. During the three years he put a loaded gun to her head three times, tried to push her out of the third story apartment window, and tried to smother her while she was sleeping. Eventually she was thrown out by him and

lived in her brother's filthy basement apartment (he had just gotten out of jail) for about two years, until she met her current husband, George. She married him to escape her miserable existence, thinking he liked her small children. Now she feels he really just fooled her.

When Louise entered counseling many years later, she was extremely tense. Her husband continually puts her down, expects her to take care of his needs, and never acknowledges that she has any needs. He promises to stop smoking marijuana but keeps on. Her son was put back into prison (where he had served time for several armed robbery episodes) due to violating parole by taking drugs again. Her oldest daughter is also involved with a physically abusive man. Louise's father, who is physically disabled, expects her to drive thirty-five miles to run errands for him because her mother refuses to help him at all. Louise has suffered from a series of serious physical ailments requiring three major surgeries in the past year. She appears to be literally falling apart, in spite of her attempts to praise God and believe that things will somehow improve.

DYNAMICS

Stressors not only differ according to their type, but they also vary with regard to their dynamics. The five key dynamics that the effective counselor must assess and address are: frequency, intensity, duration, clustering, and predictability. Stress is magnified the more frequent, intense, chronic (except for traumatic events), clustered, and unpredictable the stressors are. The American Psychiatric Association has recognized the importance of considering the severity of psychosocial stressors through the use of an Axis IV stress rating in the *Diagnostic and Statistical Manual-III-R*.[12] Their rating system involves a therapist's estimate of the combined frequency, intensity, duration, and clustering of stressors. The rating is an indication of how much stress the therapist feels that an average person might experience in similar circumstances. The stressor is classified as either an acute or enduring circumstance and is rated on a range from no stress generated to catastrophic stress.

However, the problem is still the fact that counselees may vary from the counselor, as well as from other counselees, with regard to their specific stress experience. Appendix 1 presents some suggested scales for assessing the dynamics of frequency, intensity, duration, clustering, and predictability in relation to identified stressors.

NOTES

1. J. Rotton, "The Psychological Effects of Air Pollution," (manuscript, Florida International University, 1978).

2. J. Rotton and J. Frey, "Air Pollution, Weather and Psychiatric Emergencies: A Constructive Replication," (paper presented at the American Psychological Association, Washington, D. C., 1982).

3. N. Strahilevitz, A. Strahilevitz, and J. E. Miller, "Air Pollution and the Admission Rate of Psychiatric Patients," *American Journal of Psychiatry* 136 (1978): 206–7.

4. J. Rotton, "Affective Cognitive Consequences of Malodorous Pollution," *Basic and Applied Social Psychology* 4 (1983): 171–91. Also, J. Rotton et al., "The Air Pollution Experience and Physical Aggression," *Journal of Applied Social Psychology* 9 (1979): 397–412.

5. "Outrage," in National Resources Defense Council newsletter, February 1991.

6. Julia Lawlor, "Stress, Computer Squeal Linked," *USA Today* 21 August 1990, reporting on research by Douglas Covert and Caroline Dow, Department of Communications, University of Evansville, Ind.

7. James M. Jones, "Stress at Work Takes Costly Toll," *APA Monitor* 21, no. 9 (September 1990): 37.

8. Nancy Gibbs, "How America Has Run Out of Time," *Time* 24 April 1989, 58–67.

9. Judith Wallerstein and Sandra Blakeslee, *Second Chances: Men, Women, and Children A Decade After Divorce* (New York: Ticknor and Fields, 1989).

10. Richard A. Gardner, "Childhood Stress Due to Parental Divorce" in *Stressors and the Adjustment Disorders*, ed. Joseph D. Noshpitz and R. Dean Coddington (New York: Wiley, 1990), 43–59.

11. For a thorough discussion, analysis, and counseling response to Louise's traumatic story, please refer to Craig W. Ellison and Edward S. Maynard, "Adult Children of Alcoholics," *Healing for the City: Counseling for the Urban Context* (Grand Rapids: Zondervan, 1992), 184–95.

12. American Psychiatric Association, *Quick Reference to the Diagnostic Criteria from DSM III-R* (Washington, D. C.: American Psychiatric Association, 1987), 20–21, 33–37.

Chapter Seven

Critical Choices: Temptation and the Downward Path

We have seen that as a result of flawed foundations and stressed structures formed during childhood, each person enters adulthood with a reservoir of residual stress. Those who have had particularly stressful childhoods learn to perceive and respond to their experiences in ways that create or amplify stress. Typically, they have internalized self-defeating and stress-generating beliefs and have failed to develop effective patterns of stress management. Consequently, they enter adulthood filled with residual stress. Those who have had more constructive shaping experiences have less full reservoirs. All of us carry some stress, because we have all experienced some level of ontological deficit and have chosen some paths for relief contrary to God's healthy and holy pattern for life.

Residual stress impacts *directly* upon a person's experience of stress and well-being through its shaping of personality and habit patterns. It also impacts *indirectly* as it interacts with other stressors throughout the course of later adolescence and adulthood (see figure 7.1). The combination of residual stress and current stressors results in a stress buildup that demands some form of resolution.

Stress and Choice

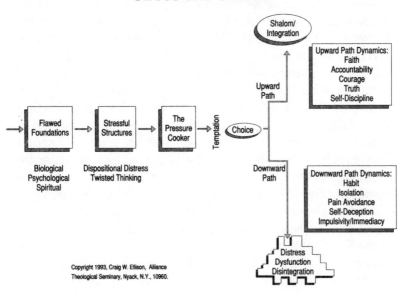

Biological   Dispositional Distress
Psychological   Twisted Thinking
Spiritual

Copyright 1993, Craig W. Ellison, Alliance
Theological Seminary, Nyack, N.Y., 10960.

Fig. 7.1

As we discussed in chapter 6, a wide variety of current biological, environmental, institutional, psychosocial, and spiritual stressors may impact upon a person (see figure 6.1, p. 83). Higher levels of residual stress cause current stressors to be experienced as more intense and overwhelming. The clustering or occurrence of multiple stressors in a short period of time especially challenges a person's coping system. Cluster stress is more likely to be experienced as overwhelming. For example, if the washer breaks down, the car needs major repairs, one of the teens gets failing grades, three kids need to be taxied to three different locations in one afternoon, and one child has a bad cold, *all at the same time,* most people will feel overloaded and are ready to fall apart emotionally or to explode in anger. If, in addition, a person carries a significant amount of residual stress from childhood due to negative self-perception, enslaving chronic emotions such as anxiety or depression, or dysfunctional controlling beliefs (such as, "A good parent has everything under control"), that individual will experience magnified stress.

The buildup of inner stress may be experienced as tension, anger, anxiety, emotional pain, shame, depression, or general distress. It is essentially the pain of unmet or threatened psychospiritual needs that has been stirred up by the current stressors. That pain demands relief.

As stress builds, it is most easy for a person to respond in more primitive, habitual, and entropic ways. This is because of the Fall, which has permanently predisposed the human race to naturally disintegrate. These choices are termed *Downward Path* choices. In the short run, they offer temporary relief from stress, but in the long run, they lead to greater pain and disintegration. The Downward Path, therefore, is deceptive and seductive. Downward Path choices reflect the entropic (disintegrative) characteristics of the entire created order subsequent to the Fall. Romans 8:20–22 describes the creation as groaning under the disintegrative impact of rampant sin and as longing for its redemption or restoration to right relationship with its Creator. Since the Fall, it has been easier to tear things down than to build things up, to destroy rather than create.

TEMPTATION

It is at the point of a person's greatest stress that Satan intensifies temptation to a maximum. Since it is his goal to destroy, he encourages people to make Downward Path choices that will eventually trap, traumatize, and tear them apart.

> **Howard** *found that he struggled greatly with the temptation to act out his homosexual urges when he was under great pressure at work and had no time to relax due to heavy responsibilities at his small church.*

The False (irrational) Self within us is especially responsive to Satan's invitations. It feeds on the *sin* (choosing in ways that contradict God's design for optimal human functioning and health) *of arrogance* (believing that one does not need to live within the boundaries of creaturely finitude but can be sovereign and unbounded, on an equal plane with God). The False Self is the egocentric, omnipotent self that resulted when the True Self was fractured at the Fall. It is self-centered rather than God-centered. It is governed by three delusional assumptions:

- I am in control or ought to be in control of all that has to do with my life.
- I am at the center of the universe.
- Everything and everyone ought to be spinning around me so I can have what I want and life will be the way I want it to be."[1]

The False Self is easily deceived into believing that lies are truth. The False Self wars against the True Self, which is the portion of the original, unified self that still reflects the image of God. The True Self is what remains in us of the original whole, healthy, rational self that reflects the image of God. Together with Satan, the False Self attempts to compel us to choose sinful, dysfunctional ways of coping with stress. Due to sin-released entropy, it is easier to do so. The result of giving in to Downward Path temptation is seductively quick relief from stress.

Temptation causes us to focus on the immediate. Thus the sin of Adam and Eve was essentially a failure of faith: they chose to be governed by their senses rather than to believe what God had told them. Similarly, Satan and the False Self attempt to convince us to listen to our physical senses and to believe that what *appears* to be true is true. They encourage us to believe that we cannot take any more pain or suffering and that we will die if we do not get relief right away. We are offered a vast array of quick fixes. Legal and illegal drugs, entertainment/sporting events, soap operas, materialism, sex, and alcohol are but a few of the more widely used ones. The problem is that these solutions are only temporary. They often leave even greater distress in a person's life because of the guilt, shame, and regret that follow in their wake. However, because they are immediately reinforcing, they are quickly turned to as stress/pain recurs. It becomes easy for a person to get trapped in a particular coping habit that solves nothing but helps one to feel good temporarily. If the habit leads to a loss of self-respect or of healthy relationships with others, such as in both chemical and nonchemical addictions, the cure will end up creating worse distress than the original pain.

Satan, of course, delights in this. No persons in their right mind would choose destruction if they knew that would be the result of the quick fix. The Scripture makes it clear, however, that Satan's two primary weapons are deception (see John 8:44—he is the father of lies and there is no truth in him; 2 Cor. 11:14—he masquerades as an angel of light) and condemnation (see Rev. 12:10—he condemns day and night). If he can deceive and seduce us into destructive coping patterns that habitually cause us to lose self-control and self-respect, while not resolving our stress, he is then able to attack us with condemnation. The False Self acts as an internal judge that picks up these charges and metes out the punishment of shame and guilt. Because we are fundamentally psychomoral beings, the pain from the shame and guilt causes greater distress. This only increases the likelihood of habitual acting out of whatever seemed to give temporary relief, in the attempt to escape from the pain of condemnation.

This, of course, is where God's grace through Christ Jesus is our salvation. His grace is able to rescue us from never-ending cycles of distress ⟶ dysfunctional choices ⟶ guilt, shame, and condemnation ⟶ greater distress ⟶ more dysfunctional choices. His grace, rather than our perfection, is the foundation of *shalom*. Psychospiritual counselors are the incarnation of God's grace. Their demeanor of caring and love toward their counselees makes it possible, little by little, for the counselees to face themselves. As they sense the counselor's acceptance and respect, they are gradually freed from the crushing grip of the "800-pound gorilla" of self-condemnation. As counselees experience and internalize grace, they are freed to begin work on healthier ways to cope with their stress.

Resisting temptation involves several steps:

1. Realizing that any choice that leads one away from or against God is a Downward Path choice.

2. Grasping the fact that quick fixes for our pain usually lead to intensified long-term pain.

3. Understanding that Satan's goal is to destroy us by deceptively entrapping us in faulty coping patterns that leave us with broken integrity and feelings of lost self-respect, guilt, and shame.

4. Knowing that when we make destructive or sinful choices, Satan encourages self-condemnation through the False Self in order to generate more pain. More often than not this leads to continued dysfunctional choices to lessen the pain of self-condemnation. This pattern eventually overwhelms and spins us out of control into the Downward Path. In order to resist temptation, we must look at it with a long-range view, be willing to suffer temporary pain, turn to God for healthy ways to meet the ontological deficits generating our pain, and realize that Satan's goal is to destroy us—not to help us with our pain and distress.

5. Realize the typical temptations that Satan directs toward us in relation to the ontological deficits that are the underlying contributors to our current distress.

Figure 7.2 lists the eight deficits and the kinds of temptations usually experienced in connection with them.

DYNAMICS

The five primary entropic dynamics that work to trap us on the Downward Path are: habit, isolation, pain avoidance, deception, and immediacy (see figure 7.3).

HABIT

Habits are an important part of human functioning that enable us to do things without spending considerable conscious energy attending to them. They are efficient, but they can also be troublesome because they are hard to change. Often the habits

Temptation and Psychospiritual Needs:
Common Temptations that Appear
When Psychospiritual Needs Are Not Met

Confusion/Identity

depression
codependency
immersion in groups
performance (doing is being)
defensive rigidity
people-pleasing
materialism
perfectionism
suicide

Loneliness/Belonging

ingratiation/compliance
initial alcohol and drug use
clinging/codependent behaviors
antisocial behavior (e.g., gang membership)
pursuit of status symbols
promiscuity, adultery
depression

Inadequacy/Competence

jealousy or envy
pride
control/domination
self-pity
despair/giving up
cheating
gossip, criticism of others
fatalism
workaholism

Rejection/Acceptance

people-pleasing/codependency
overachievement/workaholism
self-condemnation/shame
trying to achieve recognition
conformity
sexualized behaviors
withdrawal, isolation
aggression/violence

Anxiety/Security

rigidity
legalism
judgmentalism
obsessive-compulsive patterns
conformity
astrology, occult

Worthlessness/Significance

power plays
manipulation
status symbols
jealousy
malice, prejudice
greed
substance abuse
antisocial behavior
people-pleasing

Victimization/Equity

bitterness/unforgiveness
anger
hatred/revenge
self-pity
victimization/martyr's attitude
selfishness ("I'll get it for myself")
overinvolvement with rights orientation
make own rules
escape responsibilities
rebel against rules

Loss of Purpose/Transcendence

pride (like God)
occult/New Age
vain imagination
drug addiction
hopelessness
idolization
functional atheism

Fig. 7.2

formed during childhood to cope with stress are bad habits. That is, they do not effectively and wholesomely result in meeting psychospiritual needs. Instead, they result in deepened ontological deficits and lowered self-respect, shame, interpersonal alienation, and personal fragmentation. Usually, they are formed as a result of modeling the coping choices of parents under stress. They are internalized and cemented as they are tried and bring temporary relief from pain.

Habits easily become compulsive behaviors and nonchemical addictions if they bring immediate relief (positive reinforcement) from distress. Positive reinforcement strengthens the behavior associated with it, making it more likely that the behavior will be repeated. Habits such as overeating, compulsive spending, gambling, lying, hair pulling, explosive temper, prescription drug misuse, television and video game addiction, teeth grinding, irresponsible sex, and smoking[2] trap a person in a Downward Path spiral. As habitual patterns are reinforced, they begin to gain control over the person. Each repetition

Dynamics of Downward Path Movement

Habit	Automatic or conditioned responses maintained by immediate reinforcement, energy conservation, and/or ignorance of alternatives.
Isolation	Individualism; without commitment to at least one trustful and accountable relationship.
Pain avoidance	Orienting one's life and making one's choices on the bases of maximizing pleasure and minimizing pain.
Deception	False assumptions and messages; usually there are grains of truth mixed into the lie.
Immediacy	Making choices on the basis of immediate stimuli rather than on the basis of careful thought regarding long-range consequences.

Fig. 7.3

(aimed at relieving distress) results in increased pain due to the loss of self-respect, guilt, and shame over the progressive loss of self-control. The increase in pain, in turn, leads to a repetition of the habitual behavior that brings temporary relief.

ISOLATION

The tendency to withdraw from normal relationships and to become self-absorbed is called isolation. People who live in isolation find it difficult to commit to a sustained intimate relationship in which there is accountability and reciprocation. Isolation may be the result of shame and guilt.

> *Robert was a thirty-five-year-old who had great difficulty initiating relationships. He felt much more secure by himself, and yet he also felt extremely lonely. Robert carried deep feelings of shame and self-doubt within. He was afraid that other men might think he was gay (he was not) because of the way he looked, and that women would not want to be near him because of flatus (gas) that he involuntarily emitted in their presence (as a result of his self-doubt and anxiety).*

Virtually all major psychoses, serious neurotic disturbances, and addictions involve significant relational difficulties and isolation expressed either by hostility or withdrawal. Self-centeredness and self-absorption increase as a person slips down the Downward Path into more extensive psychospiritual pathology. Isolation removes accountability and correction of faulty thinking, making it easier for a person to be deceived by the False Self, to have erroneous perceptions, and to make destructive choices.

PAIN AVOIDANCE

Pain avoidance refers to a primary orientation that motivates most of one's choices. It is an attempt to avoid discomfort, pain, and suffering or to remove it quickly. It involves organizing one's life around minimizing pain.

> *Ellen was unwilling to take the risk of approaching her mother assertively and telling about some of the pain that she*

had suffered during her childhood as a result of her mother's coldness and distancing behaviors. She was also unwilling to stop an affair she was having or to stop using marijuana and cocaine because that would be too painful.

Kay had spent most of her life trying to find the easy (painless) way out. She had regularly cheated in high school and frequently took sick days from work when she was not sick. She always promised to do things others asked so that she would not risk making people unhappy, but she seldom followed through because of the effort it took.

Pain-avoiders are convinced that they cannot handle even moderate levels of distress. So they search for whatever quick fixes seem to work. They view themselves as vulnerable rather than hardy.

DECEPTION

As has been suggested in our discussion of temptation, deception is a key characteristic of Downward Path living. People who are well along the Downward Path deceive themselves and others. The ego-defenses of denial, repression, and projection are common expressions of self-deception. These ego-defense mechanisms make it appear to a person that he or she has no problem and thereby prevent any correction or change to occur due to resistance.

Marie has a serious drinking problem that she vehemently denies. Yet her drinking is causing significant conflict with her husband, who is a recovering alcoholic. Marie insists that she is not going to stop drinking until she wants to because this is one area of her life that she will not let her husband control. Besides, she maintains, he is just pointing a finger at her so that he can avoid dealing with his own problems. As long as Marie has this orientation, marital counseling with the couple will go nowhere.

Other forms of deception include false controlling beliefs that may sound correct but, when taken to an extreme, are dysfunctional and stress-generating. For example, Janelle came in for counseling due to chest pains that her doctor had concluded were due to stress. It soon became clear that several rotten family rules were the source of her stress, including "Don't make people unhappy (or they'll reject you)." These rules led Janelle to be highly nonassertive, to deny her real thoughts and feelings, and as a result, to be slowly filled with resentment. On the surface, what could be wrong with such a rule? It sounds civil; it even sounds Christian. The problem is that it is not correct. Just because people are unhappy does not mean they will reject you. Also, such a rule is imbalanced and leads to unhealthy passivity as Janelle did whatever it took not to displease anyone. In the process she gave up her own identity, which in turn negatively affected her ability to establish healthy intimacy with other family members or with boyfriends.

IMMEDIACY

The person who walks on the Downward Path focuses on the present. The current distress and immediately apparent solutions fill this person's awareness. These people find it difficult to step back from the pain and assess the implications of their choices. Rather, they tend to be impulsive and compulsive, driven either by the moods and attractions of the moment or compelled by inner urges. They are shortsighted and trapped by the options that immediately present themselves. They are totally focused and fixated on what is in front of them right now. If it is pain, they want to get rid of it—right now. If it is relief or pleasure, they want to experience it—right now. While choosing the Downward Path, they do not strategize (plan steps ahead of time) so that they can prepare themselves for temptations and vulnerable situations. As a result, they are controlled by their immediate environment.

OUTCOMES

The most powerful immediate result of choosing the Downward Path is relief from stress. This outcome is highly reinforcing and encourages repetition of the specific choices. The long-term consequences, however, are greater distress, disintegration, and even death. A useful slogan for Downward Path choices is: "Short-term gain/long-term pain." Downward

Path choices are faulty attempts to meet underlying existential deficits and to relieve the stress stemming from those unmet psychospiritual needs.

Figure 7.4 shows one way of organizing some of these unhealthy responses. Responses in the figure are categorized according to whether the people in pain are moving against, toward, or away from the perceived source of pain, as well as according to the underlying deficit. If they try to handle the distress of rejection by protesting against the perceived source of pain, for example, they will most likely express anger and blaming. On the other hand, if they try to overcome the pain of rejection by somehow influencing the perceived sources to change their responses toward themselves, they may become a codependent. Finally, if they just give up and withdraw in response to rejection, they will most likely be highly noncommunicative and may engage in a variety of nonrelational addictions. When we see certain response patterns characterizing our counselees, figure 7.4 can give us clues as to the major sources of their distress and the primary way they are trying to handle it.

If sin is viewed as those conscious and unconscious choices that are contrary to God's intended design for optimal human functioning, the Downward Path is described by such biblical comments as: "The truly righteous man attains life, but he who pursues evil goes to his death" (Prov. 11: 19); "There is a way that seems right to a man, but in the end it leads to death" (Prov. 14:12); "For the wages of sin is death . . ." (Rom. 3:23). Although these Scriptures are primarily referring to spiritual death, the consequences of Downward Path choices also include psychological and interpersonal disintegration. These consequences occur not only as a result of one's own Downward Path choices, but also when emotionally significant others make these choices, which produces or deepens the existential deficits in another person. This is an important factor in understanding the accumulation of developmental (residual) stress, which contributes to the overall buildup of stress in an adult.

Among the more serious psychosocial effects of persistent Downward Path choices are a wide variety of addictive behaviors, anxiety disorders, dysfunctional behaviors, nonorganic

Unhealthy Responses to Existential Deficits

	Protest (moving against)	Persuasion (moving toward)	Resignation (moving away)
nonacceptance (rejection)	anger; blaming/projection; bitterness	people pleasing; sexual and relationship addictions	self-doubt; extreme shyness; alcoholism and other impersonal addictive behaviors
nonbelonging (loneliness)	paranoia; rejection of the closed group	conformity/compliance; joining behavior (ingratiation);	withdrawal; depression; loneliness; alienation
incompetence (inadequacy)	jealousy; envy; sabotage of others	overcompensation; overidentification with those holding power (e.g., the boss/employer)	withdrawal; shyness; fatalism; refusal to take risks that could bring change
inequity (victimization)	rebellion/reaction against source of inequity	leading reform movements (organizing protests)	victimization mentality; bitterness
nonidentity (confusion)	rebellion; multiple personality; bizarre behaviors; eating disorders; aggressive exercise of authority	excessive conformity; rigidity; idolizing and overidentification	diffusion; lack of commitment; indecisiveness; codependency
insecurity (anxiety)	Intense efforts to control environment and others; judgment of those perceived to be untrustworthy; paranoia	rituals and construction of rigid traditions (persuading self)	anxiety; phobias; obsessive-compulsive disorders; psychosis
nonsignificance (worthlessness)	antisocial behavior; delusions of grandeur; leading protest movements	pursuit of achievement; affluence	depression; social withdrawal/isolation
nontranscendence (immediacy)	rejecting God and the spiritual; heavy use of religious authority and power	building kingdoms to rule; occultic involvement; drug use domain	suicide (e.g., Sartre); atheism; rejection of the religious

Fig. 7.4

mood disturbances, personality disorders, psychoses, and sexual disorders. These disorders occur as a result of distress—either generated or amplified by intense and unmet existential deficits—that is not addressed in ways consistent with biblical standards of wholeness (healthy and holy living). This stress model is assumed to apply only with regard to disorders that are not primarily biogenic (biochemically or organically originated).

Addictions, which result from repeated use of powerful reinforcers that quickly relieve stress and give temporary feelings of relief or euphoria, may be chemical or nonchemical. Although some experts hotly debate the possibility of nonchemical addictions, it seems quite clear that the same psychological pattern or addictive cycle occurs with a wide variety of attachments. People can become addicted to almost anything!

Anxiety disorders may be expressed in a panic disorder (with or without agoraphobia), social phobia, simple phobia, obsessive-compulsive disorder, post-traumatic stress disorder, or generalized anxiety disorder.[3]

Dysfunctional behaviors include individual and interpersonal patterns that block a full sense of satisfaction with life or with one's relationships or that are egocentric and insensitive toward the needs and desires of others. These include:

argumentativeness/aggressiveness

extreme attempts to control others

extensive use of social withdrawal and punitive silence

manipulation/exploitation of others

adultery/emotional affairs

extreme disorderliness

perfectionism

workaholism

cynicism/negativism

partially committed relationships

fear of failure

hedonism

physical and sexual abuse of others

codependency, and nonassertiveness

Mood disorders include manic episodes, major depressive episodes, bipolar disorders, and dysthymia in which it is not possible to establish "that an organic factor initiated and has maintained the disturbance."[4]

Personality disorders cause substantial impairment in normal functioning and considerable distress. They include paranoid, schizoid, schizotypal, antisocial, borderline, histrionic, narcissistic, avoidant, dependent, obsessive-compulsive, and passive-aggressive personality disorders.

Psychotic disorders involve major disturbances of a person's ability to perceive reality and to function in appropriate and realistic ways. Included are schizophrenia, brief reactive psychosis, schizophreniform disorder, schizoaffective disorder, shared paranoid disorder, psychotic depressive reaction, and manic episodes with psychotic features.

Sexual disorders include exhibitionism, fetishism, frotteurism, pedophilia, sexual masochism, sexual sadism, transvestic fetishism, voyeurism, sexual desire disorders, sexual arousal disorders, and sexual pain disorders.

In summary, the long-term consequences of Downward Path choices are distress, dysfunction, disintegration, and destruction.

NOTES

1. John E. Keller, *Let Go, Let God: Surrendering Self-Centered Delusions in the Costly Journey of Faith* (Minneapolis: Augsburg, 1985), 32.

2. These "habits" (compulsive behaviors or addictions) are addressed with simple, step-by-step directions for gaining control over them in Nonie Birkedahl, *The Habit Control Workbook* (Oakland, Calif.: New Harbinger, 1990).

3. See American Psychiatric Association, *Diagnostic and Statistical Manual of Mental Disorders*, 3d. rev. ed. (Washington, D. C.: American Psychiatric Association, 1987); William H. Reid and Michael G. Wise, *DSM-III-R Training Guide* (New York: Brunner-Mazel, 1989); and Robert L. Spitzer et al., *DSM-III-R Case Book* (Washington, D. C.: American Psychiatric Press, 1989) for descriptive, diagnostic, and intervention details regarding specific expres-

sions of anxiety, (nonorganic) mood, personality, psychotic, and sexual disorders.

4. American Psychiatric Association, *Quick Reference to the Diagnostic Criteria from DSM-III-R* (Washington, D. C.: American Psychiatric Association, 1987), 126.

Chapter Eight

Critical Choices: The Upward Path

IN CONTRAST TO THE DOWNWARD PATH, Upward Path choices are consonant with God's design for human functioning. Upward Path choices lead to a sense of completeness or wholeness, rather than psychological, relational or spiritual fragmentation. They result in a consistent (though not perfect) meeting of psychospiritual needs, resulting in *shalom*. When people make Upward Path choices, they choose to function within God-given boundaries for healthy living. Upward Path choices are more difficult to make because they do not rely on quick fixes to avoid pain, and they go against the natural entropy of our fallen world. In fact, as we shall see, effort and some level of suffering are both a necessary part of growing into maturity and ultimate well-being.

DYNAMICS

The five key dynamics underlying Upward Path choices and outcomes are parallel and inverse to the Downward Path dynamics. They are faith, accountability, courage, truth, and self-discipline (see figure 8.1). To the extent that the counselor can motivate counselee commitment to these qualities, consistent Upward Path choices will result.

FAITH

In a counseling context, faith begins with the counselee believing that it is possible for his or her future to be different from the past. It is a belief in the possibility of change. Such faith is encouraged by counselor responses that communicate a belief in the capacity of the counselee to change given sufficient understanding, commitment to therapeutic risk, patience, good

Dynamics of Upward Path Growth

Faith	Looking beyond immediate negative circumstances and problems to find reason for hope. Rooted in trust in God and aided through reframing.
Accountability	Ongoing relationship with one or more persons in which there is open sharing of needs, goals, dysfunctional behaviors, and sin, with help received in the form of prayer, challenge, guidance, and listening.
Courage	Acting according to principle, to do what is right (holy and healthy) in spite of potential or actual pain experienced in the process.
Truth	Self-perception and controlling assumptions about life, relationships, and God that are accurate and consistent with God's intended design for human functioning and are not the product of false information or deception.
Self-discipline	Pursuing a path of development that normally requires sustained effort but ultimately results in greater health and well-being.

Fig. 8.1

choices, the willingness to keep on, and the trust that God is at work in the person and will complete his good work (see Phil.1:6; 1 Thess. 5:23–24).

A faith posture is aided immeasurably as the psychospiritual counselor and counselee are able to believe that, because of God's commitment to the counselee, there is a "hope and a future" (Jer. 29:11). Faith is hanging onto the possibilities of change. It is believing that one *can* make it through the pain of saying *no* to Downward Path choices without being destroyed. It is believing that by following the guidelines God gives and by living within those boundaries one's psychospiritual needs will be met and one will experience well-being. Within the counseling situation, it is believing that the path and outcomes described by the counselor are true even though one has not chosen the Upward Path enough to experience the positive outcomes. It is the counselee trusting the counselor enough to act in ways consonant with the insight and understanding gained through the counseling process.

Faith often develops within the context of counseling, as the counselee experiences interaction with a person who is caring, competent, respectful, sensitive, and hopeful. For many this will be their first experience of such compassion. Confidence in the counselor will give counselees strength to take risks and make changes, as they experience the consistent support and faith of the counselor.

ACCOUNTABILITY

The second key dynamic for Upward Path living is accountability. Psychospiritually healthy people are not isolated. Rather, they conduct their lives as responsible members of interpersonal networks. They form nondependent and nonexploitative relationships with others. They do not view themselves as laws unto themselves. Rather, they recognize that their choices and behaviors have varying impacts upon other people. They are also aware of the power of their ego-defense mechanisms and their False Self to deceive them and encourage them to behave in ways that are not emotionally, relationally, or spiritually healthy. As a result, they establish relationships of accountability in which they honestly share their goals, their values, their struggles and failures, and their victories. They give permission to those with whom they are accountable to address concerns and apparent inconsistencies and to question them regarding their progress toward goals. They give each other permission to express feelings and forbidden thoughts in an atmosphere of acceptance—free from condemnation and rejection. They pray together.

Because of the levels of self-revelation involved, such accountability does not usually stretch beyond one or two other people. Except for a spouse, the accountable partner should be of the same sex. Partners should commit to face-to-face interaction at least once a week and should be available for phone contact at any time their partner is in need.

Self-help groups with larger numbers of people who are anonymous (various Twelve-Step groups such as Alcoholics Anonymous) or with specific sharing purposes (e.g, victims of incest; recently divorced wives) are variations of accountability. They are often useful complements to individual counseling. In the years ahead, I hope that more churches will utilize biblically based groups to encourage healthy psychospiritual accountability. It is important, though, that such groups not be places where people are concerned about being religiously correct and acceptable and as a result will not share their real hurts for fear of being rejected as inferior believers.

COURAGE

The third Upward Path dynamic, courage, is the determination to act according to principled purpose, in spite of potential or actual suffering encountered in the process. Courage is doing what is right regardless of possible pain. It is the willingness to be vulnerable in order to reach the highest qualities of human character and relationship.

Courage is the opposite of an orientation of self-protection and pain-avoidance. Those who take steps of courage are willing to risk and experience pain if it is necessary. They do not organize their lives around avoidance of stress. Courage is often expressed in the decision to seek counsel, in a counselee's willingness to try things suggested by the counselor, in the perseverance necessary to endure the temporary pain of denying

powerful Downward Path/False Self urges, and in facing the
truth about one's problems as that truth is revealed in the counseling process.

Courage is the willingness to experience the short-term pain
of taking up our particular cross (distress stemming from existential deficits and immediate stressors) and denying our False
Self, in order to experience the long-term gain of *shalom*. Just
as Christ endured the pain of the cross for the joy that was set
before him (see Heb. 12:2) and subsequently received his reward, we are to follow his example. As we fix our eyes on
Jesus, we receive strength to say *no* to the Downward Path,
even though it feels like we are dying in the moment of choice.
Indeed, part of us (the False Self) *is* dying at the moment that
we choose the path of courage. As we courageously choose and
hold onto the promise of long-term *shalom*, we are gradually
and deeply healed.

Courage is foregoing the immediate relief of quick fixes that
do not tackle the causes of one's stress and ultimately create
greater pain because they are contrary to God's design for
healthy functioning. Courage is not giving in to the pull of an
addiction, not caving in under the tyranny of anxiety, initiat-
ing an interaction in spite of extreme shyness, or going contrary
to rotten rules that have prevented healthy psychospiritual
growth. It is facing the truth of one's alcoholism, narcissism,
manipulativeness, or cruelty so that change can occur instead
of denying, blaming, rationalizing, or projecting.

The truth of the matter is that it is impossible to live a consistently Upward Path life without enduring pain. Courage is
saying *no* to entropic and egocentric urges that have gained
power over us through the formation of powerful habits. Saying *no* is often a psychologically painful experience, especially
for those who have nurtured the False Self. The False Self essentially screams and throws an emotional temper tantrum
when it is told *no*.

TRUTH

Truth is at the heart of therapeutic change and Upward Path
living. Truth is agreement with reality. It is an accurate and
nondistorted representation of the way things are. Whereas

falsehood entraps and enslaves, truth liberates the human soul and spirit.

The truth is an accurate expression of the consequences following from particular patterns of choice and behavior. Truth is based on a comprehensive biblical anthropology, which provides a solid basis for countering the distortions, deceptions, and delusions of Satan, the False Self, and significant others. Truth in the inward parts strengthens and guides the self in making healthy, mature choices and alters the false controlling beliefs, self-perception, and values that enslave people in dysfunction.

SELF-DISCIPLINE

Self-discipline is a commitment to growth and self-improvement. A self-disciplined person initiates and maintains a path designed to bring benefits of health and well-being, in spite of psychological and physical inertia that must be overcome. Self-discipline is a commitment to continue behaviors necessary for development in spite of the effort and temporary discomfort encountered in the process. It requires a focus on the long-term rewards of pursuing a particular pathway. Self-discipline is not necessarily pleasant while it is being exercised, but it ultimately brings increased feelings of self-respect and well-being. This seems to be due to its linkage with the management mandate of Genesis 1:28. As a result of self-discipline we (the True Self) feel more in control of our own self and less out of control, which in turn lowers anxiety and distress levels. Self-disciplined persons are prudent and give strategic thought to their ways (see Prov. 14:8) rather than being highly compulsive or impulsive, compliant or reactive.

OUTCOMES

Short-term results of Upward Path choices may very well result in increased distress. This is due to the experience of strong emotions such as anxiety, depression, guilt, and hopelessness that are triggered as attempts are made to violate faulty filters and rotten rules and as Downward Path habits and urges are denied. It is often as though the False Self marshals emotions like the Republican Guard of Saddam Hussein in order to fiercely resist takeover of the throne by the True Self. It throws everything possible at the True Self to try to get it to capitulate to a sense of overwhelming stress and go back to the old patterns of dysfunction and disintegration.

If the counselee, with the insightful guidance and psycho-spiritual support of the counselor and others, is able to endure the short-term suffering involved in the war between the False Self and the True Self, he or she will begin to experience a new sense of wholeness, integrity, and well-being. The counselee will begin to feel like "I'm getting it together" rather than "I'm falling apart." Although the fight to keep it together is normally lifelong for those who have greater dysfunctionality, there is usually a lessening of intensity and a sense of growing control by the True Self over time (as healthy choices continue to be made).

The counselor should respond to any relapses from the perspective of grace and mercy rather than disappointment and judgment. To respond negatively only fosters a return to the entrapping cycle of shame and destructive acting out. Encouragement and communication of belief that the counselee will overcome, with God's help, are keys for overcoming temporary setbacks and experiencing growing *shalom*. The experience of growing well-being or *shalom* is reflected in healthy relationships, psychological maturity, physical health, and spiritual well-being, which result from consistent Upward Path choices.

Shalom reflects an integrative view of human personality. It is used over 250 times in the Bible and is translated approximately 310 different ways.[1] The root meaning of *shalom* includes the concepts of wholeness, completeness, and harmony or well-being (see figure 8.2). In a considerable number of passages (e.g., Ps. 38:3), it even refers to bodily health. The term also implies the notion of being fulfilled and having unimpaired relationships with others.

Shalom is the integrative experience of functioning in the way that God originally intended (to the degree possible in a fallen world). It describes the experience of being at peace, in consonant relationship with God, with others, and within one's self. To the extent that we function harmoniously and consistently

Shalom

well-being

completeness

wholeness

harmony

health

fulfillment

unimpaired relationships

peace

Fig. 8.2

with divine design, the result is well-being. That well-being is expressed in healthy relationships, psychospiritual maturity, physical well-being, and spiritual well-being.

Healthy relationships both contribute to and are a result of *shalom*. Four primary characteristics of healthy relationships are that they are caring, nonmanipulative, nonsexualized, and nonconflicted. With regard to caring, the Bible urges the followers of Jesus to "love your neighbor as yourself" (Mark 12:31), and to "look not only to your own interests, but also to the interests of others" (Phil. 2:4b). We are exhorted to "do good to all people, especially to those who belong to the family of believers" (Gal. 6:10). Healthy relationships are characterized by caring both for the other person (nonselfishness) and caring for one's self (self-respect). Caring is being sensitive and responsive to the needs of others. Nonmanipulative relationships are described in Romans 12:9–10, 13–16. They do not use another person exploitatively as a means to some end other than the psychospiritual benefits of the relationship itself.

Nonsexualized relationships are ones that are focused on person-to-person encounters instead of body-to-body encounters. The focus is not on physical or genital pleasure to be received from the other person but upon the enjoyment of communication and common interests. Healthy relationships do not focus on the sexuality of others for egocentric purposes.

Sexual relationships are carefully and respectfully conducted within the guidelines of the Scriptures. Within marriage, sexuality is enjoyed as the culmination point of bonding and oneness in a relationship marked by growing psychological and spiritual intimacy. According to Scripture (see 1 Thess. 4:3–7), God's will is for us to be holy, and that centrally includes avoiding sexual immorality. Each of us is to learn how to have self-control; we are not to be swept up in passionate lust like those who do not know God.

Nonconflicted relationships does not mean that healthy relationships are conflict-free. Rather, they are not centered and caught in conflict. They are relationships that are generally marked by mutual appreciation, understanding, and creative conflict resolution. They are comparatively free of aggression, blaming, shaming, and judgment. Forgiving and asking forgiveness is the oil freely used to keep the relationship from seizing up in the rust of resentment.

Maturity is a term used somewhat interchangeably with *shalom*.

> The Old Testament emphasizes that God in his actions intends good for his people. Likewise, the good life in word and deed will lead the people to the goal of *shalom*, a concept of peace and prosperity as a divine gift. . . . The New Testament Greek word *teleios* (mature, perfect) was used by those who translated the Old Testament into Greek (the Septuagint) to render the Hebrew word *salem* (*shalom*), which means "sound, complete, whole." The stress is on the concept of being whole, perfect, or intact. . . . Maturity signifies the undivided wholeness of a person in his or her behavior (cf. Matt. 19:21; James 1:4).[2]

Figure 8.3 displays a number of qualities the Bible uses to describe maturity. As others have pointed out, spiritual and psychological maturity are highly interfaced.[3] This is to be expected from our view of human personality as integrative or systemic. The mature personality is positively oriented, self-disciplined, self-respectful, capable of sustained intimacy, interpersonally caring, balanced, nonaddictive, competent, able to endure normal levels of stress without becoming dysfunctional.

Physical well-being is promoted by Upward Path living because it is significantly less likely that a person will abuse his or her body with such substances as alcohol, cigarettes, or drugs as ways of relieving stress. It is also more likely that one who chooses the Upward Path will have the self-discipline to say *yes* to appropriate exercise, recreation, sleep, and nutrition, and *no* to a couch-potato, fat-ingesting lifestyle.

Finally, *spiritual well-being* both feeds and results from consistent Upward Path living. It is a key element in *shalom*. Both theory and a growing body of research suggest that healthy spirituality and subjective well-being are positively connected. Religion provides security, hope, meaning, and optimism.[4] People who interact with a caring and nurturing God more

Qualities of Maturity

Galatians 5:1, 22–23

inner-freedom
love
joy
peace
patience
kindness
goodness
faithfulness
gentleness
self-control

2 Peter 1:5

goodness
knowledge/wisdom
self-control
perseverance
godliness
brotherly kindness
love

Ephesians 4:13

Christ-likeness

Galatians 6:3–4

accurate self-evaluation

Fig. 8.3

extensively are more psychologically healthy.[5] A number of studies have found positive relationships between more conservative and intrinsic religiosity and various measures of well-being.[6] Over a decade of research with the Spiritual Well-Being Scale has found consistent relationships between positive spiritual experience and a variety of measures of physical, psychological, and interpersonal well-being.[7] As we draw closer to God, his presence strengthens our beings, supplies us with transcendent purpose, and gives us a sense of security. His love touches and heals places of brokenness and hopelessness. He gives hope and purpose for life.

THE PSYCHOSPIRITUAL COUNSELOR

It is the psychospiritual counselor's role to gently encourage counselees to consistently choose the Upward Path. This process includes helping the counselee to identify his or her deepest existential deficits and the faulty controlling beliefs and coping patterns that have promoted distress instead of *shalom*. The counselor works with counselees to identify more healthy, stress-reducing patterns for meeting their psychospiritual needs. This includes the modeling of dialogue and trustworthiness implicit in the counseling relationship itself. It may involve teaching specific skills. It includes the appropriate introduction of spiritual disciplines to help toward greater intimacy with Christ—the Prince of Peace and Wonderful Counselor. The Christian counselor is a source of encouragement, hope, accountability, comfort, truth, and motivation as counselees begin to courageously face their pain and make Upward Path choices. The process is most likely to be uneven, but the counselor provides love and acceptance for counselees even in moments of struggle and relapse.

NOTES

1. G. Kittle, ed., *Theological Dictionary of the New Testmanet*, trans. and ed. Geoffrey W. Bromiley, vol. 2 (Grand Rapids: Eerdmans, 1964).

2. Ray S. Anderson, *Christians Who Counsel: The Vocation of Wholistic Therapy* (Grand Rapids: Zondervan, 1990), 88.

3. Francis J. Buckley, S. J., and Donald B. Sharp, S. J., *Deepening Christian Life* (San Francisco: Harper and Row, 1987).

4. C. K. Hadaway, "Life Satisfaction and Religion: A Re-Analysis," *Social Forces* 57 (1978): 637–643; and David O. Moberg, *Spiritual Well-Being: Sociological Perspectives* (Washington, D. C.: University Press of America, 1979).

5. P. J. Watson, R. J. Morris, and R. W. Hood, Jr., "Intrinsicness, Self-Actualization, and the Ideological Surround," *Journal of Psychology and Theology* 18 (1990): 40–53; C. A. Preston and L. L. Viney, "Construing God: An Exploration of the Relationships between Reported Interaction with God and Concurrent Emotional Experience," *Journal of Psychology and Theology* 14 (1986): 319–29.

6. P. J. Watson, R. J. Morris, and R. W. Hood, Jr., "Sin and Self-Functioning, Part 2: Grace, Guilt, and Psychological Adjustment," *Journal of Psychology and Theology* 16 (1988): 270–81; L. R. Peterson and A. Roy, "Religiosity, Anxiety, and Meaning and Purpose: Religion's Consequences for Psychological Well-Being," *Review of Religious Research* 27 (1985): 49–62; B. D. Dufton and D. Perlman, "The Association between Religiosity and the Purpose in Life Test: Does it Reflect Purpose or Satisfaction?" *Journal of Psychology and Theology* 14 (1986): 42–48; J. Gartner, D. B. Larson, and G. D. Allen, "Religious Commitment and Mental Health: A Review of the Empirical Literature," *Journal of Psychology and Theology* 19 (1991): 6–25.

7. Craig W. Ellison, "Spiritual Well-Being: Conceptualization and Measurement," *Journal of Psychology and Theology* 11 (1983): 330–40; Craig W. Ellison and Joel Smith, "Toward an Integrative Measure of Health and Well-Being," *Journal of Psychology and Theology* 19 (1991): 35–48.

Chapter Nine

Foundations of Psychospiritual Counseling

The tongue that brings healing is a tree of life.

Proverbs 15:4

Numerous books have been written on the art and science of counseling. In this chapter we will consider the essentials of psychospiritual counseling. The ultimate goal of this approach is to enable a person or family unit to learn healthy and holy patterns of choice and behavior in response to the stresses of life. By healthy and holy patterns, we mean those that promote optimal interpersonal, physical, psychological, and spiritual functioning and well-being (*shalom*).

The goal of psychospiritual counseling is not to remove all distress. This is impossible given the chaos, disorder, and disintegration of the fallen world. Rather, the goal is to help people to sufficiently reduce residual and contemporary stress levels so that they are not highly disruptive and do not generate dysfunctional coping responses. In addition, psychospiritual counseling attempts to provide healthier options for the ongoing management of stress in the individual and in the interpersonal system. Psychospiritual counseling encourages people to discover and apply guidelines for living harmoniously with the intentions and design of the Creator. Living in this way brings healing and wholeness to broken lives.

Christian counseling must begin with a deep appreciation for the impact of the Fall upon human functioning. The basic twisting of sin involves not only the terrible warp of egocentricity but the disturbance of ontological givens. Sin also introduced the underlying terror of existential anxiety—a fear of being cut off from God and others in condemnation. At the heart of this anxiety is the fear of non-being. It is experienced as a sense of nakedness, utter vulnerability, and impending judgment. As a result of existential anxiety, human beings spend considerable energy trying to avoid condemnation and non-being by erecting ego defenses that prevent them from facing the pain of their own irresponsible and faulty choices. We want to see ourselves as good ("Every way of a man is right in his own eyes" Prov. 21:2 KJV). Because human beings are transcendent, they also are able to imagine life free of pain, and they strive to recover the state of original *shalom*. Unfortunately, they frequently choose paths that are contrary to God's design either due to their continuing attempt to be sovereign and go their own way or because of their finitude and lack of knowledge.

Having established the psychospiritual origins of pathology in the Fall, we must make it clear that all difficulties that people experience are not the product of specific, immediate sin or of direct spiritual causes. Historically, this kind of thinking has intruded upon Christian thought with regard to physical disease. This thinking has been consistently rebuffed. Jesus did not directly link disease with the sin of the sufferer, nor was Job's suffering due to his sin.

Even accepting the premise that all human beings are sinners does not adequately explain why people experience various emotional and interpersonal problems. Such a limited approach tends to blame the victim. It also confines the Christian counselor to devising a strictly spiritual solution to every problem, including those that are not immediately or directly due to spiritual causes. Ultimately, the Christian counselor who adheres to this approach is put into the position of saying to counselees, "If you'll just be perfect (be sinless, have more faith), you won't have problems." The assertion, strictly speaking, is correct—but is anyone perfect?

What we need is an approach that is spiritually rooted but also incorporates additional sources of specific pathology, such as modeling, reinforcement, biochemical disturbances, and trauma.

AN OPEN UNIVERSE APPROACH

An open universe model makes available both natural and supernatural dimensions of knowledge and counseling for the Christian counselor (see figure 9.1). An open universe approach to understanding human nature views human beings as made in the image of God, in contrast to the closed universe

Open Universe View of Reality and Human Functioning

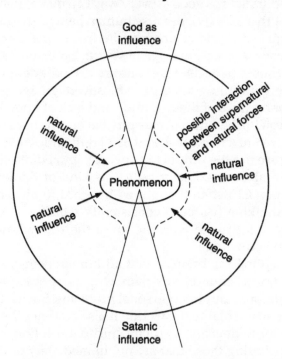

Fig. 9.1 Assumes that a given phenomenon may
be the result of either natural or supernatural
influences, or the interaction of the two.

view (see figure 9.2). The closed universe view maintains that we can know all that we need to know about reality, including human beings, through purely naturalistic, empirical investigation and explanation. That is, all that we can know is known through our physical senses. We do not need the supernatural or spiritual dimension, if it exists, to understand reality.

The open universe view holds that a complete understanding of reality requires consideration and exploration of *both* natural *and* supernatural influences. While it considers scientific study of human beings to be valid, the open universe model asserts that human nature is more than what can be empirically observed. The open universe view holds that we are best able to understand the truth by taking in both natural revelation (including scientific data) and special revelation (conveyed to the writers of Scripture and communicated to

Closed Universe View of Reality and Human Functioning

Fig. 9.2 Assumes that all phenomena can be completely explained by natural, empirically observable causes.

human understanding through the continuing activity of the Holy Spirit). This view accepts the active interaction of God with the created order, including human beings. Other spiritual influences, such as those of Satan and his demons, are also able to directly and indirectly impact upon human functioning.

This approach provides for supernatural (classic forms of pastoral care and deliverance), integrative (psychospiritual), and nonspiritual (cognitive, social learning, behavioral, biological, systemic) counseling interventions. The interventions that are chosen depend upon analysis of the origins of each counselee's pathology. Counseling based on this model is multidimensional, creative, comprehensive, and flexible. It fits the counseling to the person rather than imposing stereotypic, rigid intervention options.

HEALING AND THE WHOLE PERSON

May God himself, the God of peace, sanctify you through and through. May your whole spirit, soul and body be kept blameless at the coming of our Lord Jesus Christ. The one who calls you is faithful and he will do it.

1 Thessalonians 5:23–24

Both psychological and theological views of human personality suggest that psychospiritual health is optimal when all parts of the person are functioning harmoniously together. Holistic conceptions of healthy personality are an integral part of the personality theories of Adler, Allport, Maslow, and Rogers, among others.[1] Each of these major theorists viewed the healthy personality as one that continually moved toward greater wholeness and unity. Theological views have also promoted an integrative view of healthy personality. Consider, for example, this Hebraic viewpoint.

Spiritual holiness or emotional wholeness can be achieved only when the total self is involved. Neither holiness or wholeness will be secured if the self remains segmented, and either the *soma* or *psyche* is withdrawn from involvement in confrontation. Furthermore, neither holiness nor wholeness can be achieved through man's own efforts. The flesh (*basar*) is powerless to act. It is the spirit (*ruach*) of God who enables man to become a whole person (*nephesh*). . . . It is not the body or the mind which acts, but it is the total person.[2]

The Saxon word from which *health* is derived is the same word from which the word *whole* comes.[3] Health and wholeness are integrally related. Well-being is the result of the proper functioning as an integrated system. It is the product of the harmonious, orderly interaction of interdependent parts of a whole.

Intrapsychic and interpersonal conflict have consistently been seen as sources of emotional turmoil and mental disturbance by most contemporary theories of personality.[4] Disintegration or fragmentation produces distress and dysfunction.

The biblical view of *shalom* reflects this systemic view of healthy human personality and functioning. The root meaning of *shalom* includes the concepts of completeness, wholeness, and harmony or well-being.[5] *Shalom*, the goal of psychospiritual counseling, is the result of a person functioning as an integrated system in proper balance within and without. Human beings are unable to fully and continuously experience *shalom* because of the disordering effects of the Fall, sin, and human error. However, to the extent that they live consonantly with God's design for human functioning, they will experience higher degrees of well-being and lower levels of stress.

The holistic nature of human personality implies that the psychospiritual needs for acceptance, belonging, competence, equity, identity, security, significance, and transcendence are interdependent as well. Healthy interpersonal experience and accurate thought processes are crucial ingredients for the experience of any of the eight needs. The ultimate source of provision for these needs would be the perfect experience of perfect love.

Psychospiritual counseling aims at comprehensive and systemic understanding and engagement of the *whole person,* rather than being highly analytical, atomistic, and technical in orientation. Psychospiritual counseling is careful to address interpersonal and cognitive processes that have contributed to particular patterns of psychospiritual deficits and dysfunctional attempts at stress management. Although we will look at healing in relation to specific subparts of human personality in the remaining chapters, specific interventions are a matter of emphasis. They depend upon which psychospiritual needs have contributed to a particular person's stress.

Psychospiritual counseling is aimed at promoting emotional, relational, spiritual, and physical well-being. This reflects the holistic, systemic meaning of *shalom*.

COUNSELING AND THE HOLY SPIRIT

> *Praise be to the name of God*
> * for ever and ever;*
> *wisdom and power are his. . . .*
>
> *He gives wisdom to the wise*
> * and knowledge to the discerning.*
> *He reveals deep and hidden things;*
> * he knows what lies in darkness,*
> *and light dwells with him.*

Daniel 2:20–22

The heart of healing for the Christian counselor is the release of God's grace and power into a life that is broken. The open universe model of healing, which underlies psychospiritual counseling, suggests that the Holy Spirit, who is identified as the counselor, helper, and comforter (see John 14:16; 15:26) and the one who guides the children of God into all truth (John 16:13), acts within human experience to release support, understanding, hope, psychospiritual strength, and healing.

The Holy Spirit frequently touches Christians in need by drawing them into counseling and giving insight to identify the real problem. He also facilitates interpersonal bonding between the counselor and the counselee. This bonding stimulates counselees to have the courage to continue counseling and to make changes when their natural inclination would be to run from the pain of self-revelation. The Holy Spirit at times convicts counselees of moral infractions that are creating stress and disintegration. He is able also to provide hope and comfort, often channeled through the caring counselor.

The Holy Spirit actively interacts with the Christian counselor who seeks his presence in the counseling room. Counseling is an art as well as a science; it is therapy, not just technology. This means that there are countless decisions and diverse interventions to choose from. Counseling is not precise; it is more than a mechanical set of stereotypic procedures. As a result, the Holy Spirit (who is omniscient) is able to grant sensitivity to and accurate interpretation of deeper feelings that are only partially expressed by counselees. He also guides with regard to the proper timing of probes, therapeutic confrontation, and interpretations so that those interventions have maximum impact. The Holy Spirit grants understanding and insight into the dynamics underlying the counselee's problem. He is able to stimulate creativity, expressed in the generation and appropriate application of therapeutic imagery, metaphors, and interventions.

The healing work of the Holy Spirit is dependent upon the humility and desire of the Christian counselor for his guidance and empowering. The Christian counselor who welcomes the Holy Spirit's wisdom and healing activity must be right with God (i.e. in active communion, not harboring unresolved sin) in order to be able to sense the Spirit's leading and in order to be a clear vehicle for conveying God's healing grace.

PRAYER

The Sovereign LORD has given me
an instructed tongue,
to know the word that sustains the weary.

He wakens me morning by morning,
wakens my ear to listen like one being taught.

Isaiah 50:4.

Prayer is a natural and necessary companion of the Christian counselor. There is some debate among Christian counselors whether the counselor should pray out loud with counselees—some feel that to do so is too easily manipulative and ritualistic, while others feel that it can be helpful if used carefully and in response to God's leading. Yet there can be little debate that the Christian counselor should privately intercede for the counselee, and should pray for the counseling process and for guidance as a counselor. The Christian counselor who engages in supplication expresses dependency upon the Wonderful Counselor (Jesus Christ) and the Counselor/Comforter/Helper (Holy Spirit). The prayer of supplication recognizes one's own finitude. It can be used effectively to comfort, to give praise for progress, and to affirm some new insight.

The use of Scripture when praying with a counselee is appropriate as long as it does not involve preaching at the counselee. One of the surprising experiences that I have had is the appreciation expressed to me on several occasions when I have prayed with nonbelievers at the end of a counseling session. These counselees expressed that my prayer had somehow strengthened them and given them hope through the week or two between counseling sessions.

Finally, prayer *by* counselees should be done only if the counselee expresses the desire to pray or is considerably at ease with the thought of praying. One must *always* be careful to ask permission to pray in such a way that counselees feel comfortable to decline. Prayer by counselees can be used as a means of sealing a commitment, of establishing a new perspective, for confession and repentance, and for overcoming bitterness. The Christian counselor must be careful that the counselee does not view prayer superstitiously. That is, it must be made clear that prayer is not some sort of magical shortcut that will spare the counselee therapeutic effort or pain. Rather, it is most often a source of psychospiritual empowering for change. While prayer for comfort should be encouraged, it should again be understood that God often brings that comfort in ways that do not circumvent struggle and the need for courage.

CLIMATE OF SAFETY

*Therefore encourage one another and build each other
up, just as in fact you are doing.*

1 Thessalonians 5:11

It is critical that the Christian counselor provide a setting of security for the counselee. It is easy to forget that in a society that places a premium on self-sufficiency and individuality, just coming for help is a significant act of courage for most people. Coming in for counseling is an admission that they cannot handle their problems on their own; as a result, many people feel like failures when they enter counseling. There may be embarrassment and shame, especially as a congregant faces the pastor and begins to reveal material that seems non-Christlike and unbecoming to a believer. First-time counselees are frequently unsure about what to expect. Misconceptions of counseling abound and public mistrust of counselors has increased as headlines highlight therapists who have sexually abused their clients.

With regard to pastors who counsel, their attitudes toward people and life problems—reflected in pastor-parishioner interaction and sermons—will affect counselee feelings of safety. If the pastor seems to appreciate and enjoy people and communicates an attitude of respect for people encountering the struggles of life, counselees will be more inclined to seek the pastor out for counseling and to feel safe. If pastors distance themselves from parishioners and convey an attitude of judgment toward those who are weak (struggling with problems), most counselees will not risk being vulnerable.

The initial counseling session is always important for creating a climate of safety and for providing a framework of expectations for the counselee. First, the counselor should explain the safeguard of confidentiality. The counselee needs to be assured that the fact that the person is receiving counseling and what is shared in counseling will not be communicated to anyone else, except for preestablished exceptions. These stated exceptions to absolute confidentiality normally include:

1. Occasions when the counselee, in the counselor's professional judgment, appears to be a danger to himself or herself or to another person, and the counselor determines that additional intervention by police or through hospitalization is necessary for the sake of protection.

2. Instances of suspected child abuse. Depending upon the laws of the particular state, the counselor (including pastoral counselors) must report such suspicion to the appropriate child protective service in the state. Some states allow "reasonable suspicion," while other states mandate a report if there is *any* suspicion. Failure to report may lead to criminal charges against the counselor.

3. Situations when the counselee agrees that information needs to be reported to other parties. In these cases, the counselor should have the counselee sign a consent form granting permission for professional information to be shared to specifically named parties for specific purposes and/or for a designated time period.

It is also important for the pastoral counselor to indicate that information from current counseling will not be used as public illustrations within the church and that any illustrations used will be from past situations and will be protected by name and detail changes. Both for the pastor and the Christian therapist, it is usually best to use composites in speaking and writing or to secure explicit written permission for specific information to be used. It is best that the pastor use thoroughly veiled illustrations from *previous* ministry.

The climate of safety is also encouraged by letting your clients know that you regard human problems and human needs as a normal part of life in a fallen world. They should know that you feel everyone needs help at some point during the journey through life, and that you regard that person's willingness to come to you as a step of courage. They should be assured that they will not lose face by sharing things that might be difficult or even shameful to them. They should be encouraged to understand that you have found that God's grace is a powerful aspect of healing, and that your role is to be a vehicle for that grace to be experienced.[6] Assure them that you do not look on things that are regarded as "bad" in a condemning way but with the prayerful attitude of wanting to help bring about desired change. Having said all of this, it is *absolutely critical* that your facial expressions, posture, words, and interaction sincerely express *acceptance* of the person, even while you work with them to bring about needed, client-committed change.

KNOWLEDGE

The teaching of the wise is a
fountain of life,
turning a man from the snares
of death.

Proverbs 13:14

Although God is the Master Counselor and the Holy Spirit responds to the prayerful commitment of the Christian counselor, this is not a substitute for knowledge. Counseling is not preaching and must not be approached from an exclusively theological or spiritual angle. It is a psychospiritual intervention aimed at the whole person. It is critical that the counselor be well-versed in theory, data, and intervention approaches appropriate to those problems that are most likely to be encountered.[7] These include:

marital difficulties (communication; conflict resolution)

nonchemical addictions (sexual, fantasy, chronic buying, compulsive shoplifting)

adult children of alcoholic families/codependency

child-rearing problems

divorce and divorce recovery

single parenting

grief/loss

stress

sexual abuse (usually being revealed by adults in regard to their childhood) victims of trauma (accidents; rape; other invasive/assaultive crimes)

life/career guidance and domestic (spouse or child) abuse

The Christian counselor/pastor should be regularly reading or attending workshops to update personal understanding and skills in these areas of need. I strongly recommend that the counselor read at least one book each month as part of a life-long process of continuing professional education. Read interactively and evaluatively, with current or recent cases in mind. This will help you to assess and adapt your understanding and therapeutic process if it becomes clear that change is needed. This approach will also help you to translate more abstract material into practical terms and to better recall the material read. The most effective approach to continuing knowledge acquisition and application is to establish a common reading program with a colleague. Take an hour each month to meet and reflect on your reading as it applies to your counseling experience.

ANALYSIS

The purposes of a man's heart are
deep waters,
but a man of understanding
draws them out.

Proverbs 20:5

An essential part of counseling for *shalom* is a thorough and accurate analysis of underlying psychospiritual deficits, distorting ego defenses, damaging controlling beliefs, stress-amplifying dispositions, contemporary sources of stress, and destructive Downward Path patterns of stress management. The model presented in this book provides an effective analytical framework. Depending upon the levels of stress, the degree of personal and interpersonal disintegration, and the psychospiritual awareness of the counselee, the process of analysis will take varying lengths of time. Often, analysis is like peeling an onion. Earlier analysis, while accurate and important to the counseling outcome, may be followed by successively deeper levels of analysis and healing.

The Christian counselor needs to help counselees see the psychospiritual roots of their distress. (We also recognize the impact of the Fall upon the physical state of humans and the fact that some problems have biological origins.) This involves helping them to identify and change their most significant ontological deficits and the faulty coping patterns they have established to meet their psychospiritual needs. Often we can identify ontological deficits by understanding the emotions characteristically associated with specific deficits (see Figure 4.1, page 53).

The counselor then proceeds to use all appropriate interventions to help the counselee change those faulty coping patterns, and adopt new perceptions and ways of meeting basic needs. The goal is to help counselees cope more constructively with their stress by making choices that are consistent with God's design for human functioning. In this process, the care and compassion of the counselor is crucial. When the counselor does not reject the counselee who shares things about which he or she feels deep guilt or shame, healing grace is released into the counselee's life and stress begins to be relieved.

A counselor who actively listens and encourages self-analysis aids the accuracy, thoroughness, and pace of analysis. It is usually helpful to explain the eight ontological givens or psychospiritual ideals that we all long for and the existential deficits or psychospiritual needs that correspond to those ideals. As the counselee discusses personal developmental experiences, the counselor should listen carefully for particular deficits and reflect those observations back to the counselee for self-analysis and reaction. The counselor should pay attention to particular emotional and behavioral patterns that are likely to correspond with specific existential deficits (see figure 4.1, page 53). This same process is utilized to accurately uncover cognitive, behavioral, and dispositional (particularly of the self) distortions, which either undergird the person's psychospiritual needs or are attempts to handle the pain of experienced deficits.

To help make the process of analysis more standardized and systematic, refer to the Psychospiritual Needs Inventory (PNI), displayed in appendix 1. The PNI assesses the degree of deficit present in each of the eight ontological dimensions.[8]

CHANGE

The tongue of the wise brings healing.

Proverbs 12:18

A key role for the counselor is to encourage change. While change is only one of several counseling purposes (comfort, guidance, and support are others), a significant amount of counseling is concerned with changing perception, thoughts/meanings, behaviors, goals, interactions, and emotions that are somehow inadequate and have hindered optimal well-being. The counselor must determine *with* the counselee what changes are necessary and what degree of counselee commitment to making those changes is necessary to promote *shalom*.

Change is facilitated by hope, transmitted to the counselee through interaction with the counselor. As counselees sense that the counselor believes in them, in their potential and worth, and in their ability to make changes, counselee motivation and self-perception are enhanced in such a way that change becomes possible.

Christine wept for almost the entire first counseling session. She had been crying for much of the preceding two weeks. She felt that God had played a cruel joke on her in all areas of her life. She felt hopeless and depressed. She was tired of trying to please people and was on the verge of leaving her husband of twenty years who had taken her for granted, until the current crisis. Forced out of her position as an executive, she felt trapped with nothing to do, no status; she felt alienated from God and resented her husband. She had consistently hidden deep emotional pain in workaholism.

As therapy proceeded, it became evident that pleasing and performing had been the two primary patterns she had used to cope with constant rejection from her parents, who communicated verbally and nonverbally that she was an unwanted burden and had consistently invalidated her needs and perspectives. She had tried to get rid of her sense of "bad self" by giving her self away and by pleasing people. But now, through a combination of events, including severe physical problems that were clearly the result of the chronic stress she had been under as she desperately tried to pretend that everything was okay, she realized that her former strategy no longer worked.

Through counseling Christine became aware of the counselor's hope for her. She began to understand that she was an acceptable person who did not need to please or perform, and her sense of desperation and helplessness began to lessen. Gradually, she let herself believe that her parents were unloving and wrong, and that she was worth being loved without vacating herself and pretending to be whatever she thought others wanted her to be. She was able to express her anger to God and to her husband and to begin building assertive relationships with them that enhanced her sense of positive identity.

CHOICE

It is for freedom that Christ has set us free. Stand firm, then, and do not let yourselves be burdened again by a yoke of slavery.

Galatians 5:1

Many of those who enter counseling feel trapped and without options. They feel, like Christine, that God and others have conspired against them and that all they can do is fatalistically accept their miserable lot in life. Many *want* to be freed from emotional and addictive prisons but feel they do not have the ability or strength to choose a better way.

On my window sill is a small sign that says "Choice, not destiny." This was a thank-you gift to me from a client who entered therapy highly depressed. She believed there was no

future and that God did not want her to live much longer.
Pauline *had been physically and verbally abused throughout childhood by her father, who basically blamed her for whatever went wrong in his life. Through therapy, Pauline began to discover that her depression was responsive to the choices that she made. If she immersed herself in certain thought patterns and engaged in a chaotic lifestyle, she would become depressed. As she disciplined her thinking, told God what she was feeling, and chose to be a proactive participant in life, she began to feel better. The key for her healing, which went through a series of ups and downs as she learned these critical lessons, was her choices. She learned that her present and future did not have be a replication of her past.*

(It is important to note that some depression is primarily biochemically based, making therapeutic change through conscious choice very difficult without some degree of companion drug treatment as well.)

The perception of one's ability to make choices that make a difference is critical for much therapeutic progress. The development of the belief that one *can* choose a different way and *can* change is crucial. The belief that one does not have to remain imprisoned by the past or by one's perspectives is highly motivating. It is the counselor's role to help the counselee become aware of optional patterns of perceiving, choosing, and acting, as well as to support the person through the inevitable ups and downs of the change process. As the counselor continues to stress the counselee's ability to choose and reinforces healthy decision-making, even when there are slips and setbacks in the process, the counselee is empowered to make changes.

Distress began with a sinful choice in the Garden, but *shalom* is the result of good decision-making. Every time a person is faced with the buildup of pressure, that individual is given the opportunity to choose the Upward or Downward Path. The counselor's role is to encourage Upward Path choices that are likely to increase short-term pain but bring long-term emotional, relational, spiritual, and physical gain (well-being). Though ingrained habits militate against good decision-making, it is possible for a person to choose constructively with enough support.

STRATEGIZING

The teaching of the wise is
a fountain of life,
turning a man from the snares
of death.

Proverbs 13:14

Therapeutic change is not so much a matter of willpower (although self-discipline is important) as it is a matter of effective strategy. In strategizing the counselor helps the counselee set goals, establishes goal paths with specific tasks, evaluates motivation and counselee commitment to the strategy, anticipates and discusses possible points of difficulty and relapse, and insures both accountability and encouragement for the counselee on a continuing basis, as needed. Strategizing takes into account the counselee's past attempts at change; it examines what was attempted and what failed.

Often a person or couple will indicate that they experienced success for a while, as a result of past counseling, but that "something happened . . . we don't know what . . . we just seemed to slip back into the old ways." I am increasingly convinced of the need to teach individuals and couples to use short-term renewable contracts to overcome the natural human tendency toward entropy.

Bill and Hannah came for counseling, complaining that their love for each other had grown cold and they wanted to change that. Over a number of sessions I guided them in developing a strategy, which was then described in a detailed, renewable contract. They found that a monthly review of their specific commitment, followed by each reading the contract aloud and re-signing it for the following month, helped them to stay on target and restored the feelings of love that they had lost. They had the option to revise or not renew the contract at any point, and if doing this created any difficulties between

*them, they were encouraged to return to the counselor for help
in negotiation.*

Similar contracts are also helpful during intermediate stages
of counseling people trapped in addictions. At a point in the
counseling process (usually several months into it) when the
counselee has made a commitment to recovery but has been
inconsistent in overcoming the addiction and has been consistently accountable and honest with the counselor, a time-
specific, experimental contract can be established. In the
contract, the counselee commits to not engage in the addictive
behavior but to use specific alternative ways of coping that are
part of the overall change strategy. The contract should be discussed thoroughly and regarded as experimental (to reduce
possible backlash of shame if there is failure). Issues that might
make it difficult for the counselee to follow through should be
discussed, and it should be determined that the counselee is
highly motivated to work the agreement.

> **Glenn,** *a married adult in his thirties who had a sexual
addiction involving cross-dressing and masturbation, found
that two-week renewable contracts provided the extra boost of
strength and confidence he needed, together with other compo-
nents of his strategy that provided alternatives and outs, to
sustain his recovery.*

The process of strategizing usually promotes hope as the
counselee begins to feel that he or she is not helplessly caught
in a sea of chaotic urges and emotions that control and leave
one impervious to change. Rather, as a plan is carefully laid
out with graduated steps of likely success and with consistent
counselor support, even in the face of temporary setbacks, the
counselee is strengthened to believe that change can and will
occur. As the strategy begins to work, counselees are encouraged to believe that they *can* walk on the Upward Path and are
not doomed to disintegration and destruction.

NOTES

1. L. A. Hjelle and D. J. Ziegler, *Personality Theories: Basic Assumptions, Research, and Applications* (New York: McGraw-Hill), 1981.

2. G. E. Whitlock, "The Structure of Personality in Hebrew Psychology," in *Wholeness and Holiness*, ed. H. Newton Malony (Grand Rapids: Baker, 1983), 48. (Reprinted from *Interpretation* 14 [1960]: 3–13).

3. J. A. Sanford, *Healing and Wholeness* (New York: Paulist, 1977).

4. S. R. Maddi, *Personality Theories: A Comparative Analysis* (Homewood, Ill.: Dorsey, 1976).

5. G. Kittel, ed., *Theological Dictionary of the New Testament*, trans. and ed. Geoffrey W. Bromiley, vol. 2 (Grand Rapids: Eerdmans, 1964).

6. David Seamand, *Healing Grace* (Wheaton: Victor, 1988) provides excellent psychological and biblical understanding of the powerful role of grace in human healing.

7. See Craig Ellison and Edward Maynard, *Healing for the City* (Grand Rapids: Zondervan, 1992) for a helpful resource section of books and organizations dealing with the ten problems pastors and Christian counselors most frequently encounter.

8. Those interested in collaborative test construction and research on the Psychospiritual Needs Inventory are invited to contact Dr. Craig W. Ellison at Alliance Theological Seminary, 122 South Highland Avenue, Nyack, New York 10960 or at New Hope Counseling Center, 68–60 Austin Street, Suite 301, Forest Hills, New York 11355. This will become a companion instrument to the Spiritual Well-Being Scale (see chapter 12) and the Spiritual Maturity Index also constructed by the author.

Chapter Ten

Emotional Well-Being

As we have already seen, *SHALOM* implies the concept of whole person maturity and well-being. The Christian counselor intervenes in order to promote emotional, relational, spiritual, and physical well-being. Psychospiritual healing occurs throughout the human personality because human beings are integrated systems. In this chapter we will specifically examine counseling interventions that promote emotional maturity and well-being.

Emotional well-being is a reflection of healthy nurturing, modeling, and discipline during childhood. Those who have been reared in a climate of love and acceptance are more likely to display qualities of emotional maturity. Those who have observed parents and other adult models who were emotionally healthy, positive, and appropriate are more likely to be emotionally whole as adults. Those who were disciplined assertively, with an emphasis on correction and teaching instead of on punishment and pain, show greater levels of emotional maturity. Those who have entered adulthood with positive feelings about themselves demonstrate the greatest degree of emotional well-being.

Unfortunately, fragmentation, condemnation, and distortion of the person were among the initial effects of the Fall. The resultant struggles that people have with issues of *identity* and *self-esteem* are among the most common and toughest issues the Christian counselor will face.

IDENTITY

Struggles with identity include: (1) anxiety and confusion over the right to think and feel as a being separate from emotionally significant others; (2) lack of clarity and connection with one's own thoughts and feelings; and (3) confusion or false beliefs about one's place and purposes in life.

> *Frances, a pleasant woman in her late thirties, was well-liked by everyone. People frequently sought her help and she was always willing to comply. She lived with her parents, who depended on her for many of their needs. Although she had been married for about four years during her mid-twenties, her ex-husband abused her physically, engaged overtly in several affairs, and finally left her. She entered counseling feeling confused, anxious, and victimized.*
>
> *Lori came in to talk when she learned that her father had sexually touched her sister-in-law when he gave her a backrub. Two of Lori's sisters also reluctantly revealed that during their youth their father had sexually molested them. The family regarded themselves as very close. When they were growing up, family togetherness was emphasized. Bedroom doors were expected to be open and the bathroom door unlocked. Father made a habit of giving his girls baths until they were seven or eight years old. As they grew older, he continued to give them backrubs. When he lost his job, he and his wife went to live for several months at a time with each of the children in turn but did not offer to help with any of the expenses they incurred.*

In both of these cases there was considerable confusion over appropriate boundaries between self and significant others.

Both Lori's siblings and Frances had learned that they were essentially extensions of the egos of significant others. They became what was expected of them by others. They had no definitive line of distinction between themselves and others, thus they were not consciously aware of their right (need) to have private, separate, physical, and psychological space in order to have a sense of self as God intended. Only when frightening feelings and disturbing experiences occurred did they began to admit that something was wrong. Their first reaction was to blame themselves and try to figure out how they should have acted differently.

Because these women were Christians, counseling intervention began with an examination of biblical perspectives on individual identity and familial enmeshment. For example, although Adam and Eve were made to be in close relation with each other, they had separate identities. Psalm 139 emphasizes God's caring awareness for the individual from before conception. Jesus' declaration of his individuality and separate identity when he stayed behind at the temple (to the consternation of his parents) further encourages the legitimacy of a sense of self separate from a parent or from emotionally significant others.

Those struggling with identity issues must understand that they have internalized rotten rules that make them feel like they are traitors and terrible beings if they attempt to differentiate themselves. As a result they become submerged personalities. The psychospiritual counselor must help these individuals understand some of the possible reasons why an emotionally significant other has encouraged them to be so enmeshed and submerged. This can be done by using a genogram[1] to trace possible family history factors in their parents' experience in light of the eight psychospiritual needs suggested in chapter 2 (see pages 13 and 22, and fig. 1.1).

The counselor should gradually encourage the counselee to take steps to differentiate from others. This initially involves a thorough discussion of the counselee's deepest fears about becoming a separate self. The counselee must come to the point of being able to risk incurring the feared consequences. The counselor can encourage the counselee to objectify his or her fears by examining the likelihood of the feared consequences.

The counselor also helps the counselee to plan how to respond in the face of the most significantly feared outcomes. A process of assertiveness is then initiated. This is best done in a series of steps that are initially low-key and nonconfrontational, but that eventually may require more direct assertion of self.

As those steps are taken, the counselee should be made aware that he or she will initially experience a variety of negative feelings as a result of violating inner rules of self-submersion. These will probably include feelings of anxiety, guilt, treachery, and disloyalty. The counselee needs to anticipate these feelings and understand that after those feelings, which act like soldiers trying to maintain the status quo, good feelings will start to emerge from deep within. Those good feelings are feelings of self-respect, integrity, and esteem—the natural products of a healthy sense of self and of appropriate self-assertion.

A second set of identity issues involves difficulty in being able to connect with one's *own* thoughts and feelings. This is likely to be the result of socialization patterns that have de-emphasized inner awareness or discouraged expression of intimate feelings and thoughts. As we have mentioned in our discussion of gender in chapter 4, men are typically more handicapped in this area than women. Most boys are taught to focus outside of themselves, to ignore and deny emotion, and to focus their communication and friendship on more impersonal and external issues.

> *When Joe came in for counseling, the only feeling that he could identify and express was "frustrated" or "frustrating." He applied that label to virtually everything. We began a process of emotional language acquisition with Joe. It was a slow and painstaking process, but gradually he was able to describe his daily experiences with a number of different emotions.*
>
> *Joe had come from a culture and family that never showed emotion. His mother expressed very little affection toward him, and his parents were both emotionally flat. He learned that it was "bad" to have and to express feelings, so he shut down emotionally. Joe admitted to being numb inside, especially since his wife had walked out on him fifteen years ago.*

I introduced Joe to an extensive list of feeling words.[2] *He agreed to work with three of the words each week. His assignment was to (1) write down a few words or phrases describing what each feeling feels like; (2) briefly describe his experiences with that feeling (if any); (3) share this information with the counselor. At first, Joe came up empty-handed. I shared a number of feelings with him, giving him my description and experience, and asked him if he could remember ever having such an experience. Gradually, Joe was able to generate these on his own.*

This assignment does not produce dramatic immediate results, but over time it can enrich people's emotional vocabulary and help them to get in touch with themselves. It can also be used effectively to build more intimate communication between marriage partners, particularly in cases where one or both partners have difficulty expressing emotions.

A third set of identity issues involves confusion or false beliefs about one's purposes and place in life.

Ben's parents had told him in a variety of ways that he was retarded and was not able to live and choose for himself. When he came to me, he was in his late twenties and was still living with his parents. He had gone to a community college about ten years earlier, but he flunked out during his first year due to a combination of dyslexia and low self-confidence. He worked as a janitor and was filled with self-doubt and feelings of worthlessness. He did not feel capable of doing anything competently, but he did have a special love for senior citizens. With encouragement from his church, he had begun to reach out to the elderly in his community in a variety of practical ways.

During counseling, Ben began to see that the messages he had been given about his capabilities and significance were wrong. His confusion about himself (which included questions about homosexuality since he did not dare reach out to women for fear of painful rejection) began to clear. He began to realize that people all around him in his church and community were affirming him for his caring and effective outreach to seniors. As he began to connect with these true messages, he committed himself, with my support, to several practical steps of self-improvement. Eventually, he returned to college to further his career goal of working with senior citizens.

Ben's whole sense of self changed dramatically during his two years in counseling. Even his parents began to realize they had seen him wrongly and began to affirm him.

GUILT, SHAME, AND SELF-ESTEEM

Guilt and shame are the products of judgment. They are expressions of the ontological deficit of rejection. In the case of guilt, a person feels bad or judged because he or she has done something that violates a public or private standard. The standard may be a just standard, reflecting God's rules for proper living, or it may be an arbitrary standard that is the result of a particular socialization process.[3] Nevertheless, guilt is a failure to keep the standard.

Shame is related to guilt but is associated with feelings that one is defective or bad in one's inner being. Among the self-thoughts of those who are filled with shame are such beliefs as being a mistake, flawed, dirty, ugly, disgusting, not good enough, unloved, small, awful, contemptible, nothing, deserving of criticism, embarrassed, and humiliated.[4]

Guilt and shame are closely associated with deficits in self-esteem. Counseling needs to aim not only at reducing guilt and shame but also at building a biblically grounded sense of self-worth.[5]

Counseling intervention aimed at reducing guilt and shame and promoting positive self-esteem includes helping counselees to take the following steps.

1. *Sort out true and false guilt.*

Anthony had tremendous feelings of guilt whenever he had to turn down one of his widowed mother's requests for help. Coming from an Italian family, loyalty to his parents had been deeply internalized. The problem was that his mother's many requests were more like demands. Helping her had begun to take more and more of his time, which made it difficult for him to

*get his own work done. This resulted in growing resentment
from his wife. Whenever he said "no" to his mother, she had a
way of letting him know that he had let her down, and he felt
intense guilt.*

False guilt is culture- or family-based. Instilling guilt is often practiced as a way of controlling children (who become
adults). As a result, false guilt is closely related to shame because it encourages people to feel bad about what they have
done and even about themselves. True guilt, on the other hand,
is based on biblical standards of right and wrong. Before God,
we are all (judicially) guilty. As Bruce Narramore points out,
however, the appropriate, God-given response to true guilt is
godly sorrow and repentance, not guilt feelings.[6]

2. *Receive God's forgiveness and forgive themselves.* As long as
people wallow in guilt or shame, punishing themselves for
their transgressions or awfulness, there can be no healing of the
self. Because those who struggle with guilt and shame often
internalize perfectionistic standards, anything less than perfection is proof of their need to be condemned. They can neither
accept God's forgiveness nor forgive themselves because of the
awfulness of their actions (guilt) or being (shame). They feel
they deserve punishment, not pardon, because they are not
perfect.

The counselor can begin to give permission for receiving forgiveness by his or her own interaction with counselees. As
counselees see that the counselor does not shrink back from
them or convey judgment, and yet fully recognizes their
"awfulness," they are encouraged to begin changing their self-
condemnation. As the psychospiritual counselor begins to
share Scripture regarding the grace of God in light of his un-
compromising holiness, and as counselees ponder God's
accepting and forgiving responses toward such biblical char-
acters as David (adultery, murder), Rahab (prostitute in
Christ's geneological line), and Paul (murderer, "chief of sinners"), false guilt and shame begin to melt away. As counselees
understand that God has already forgiven their true (judicial)
guilt through Christ's death on the cross, they begin to see that
further self-crucifixion is unnecessary.

It is important to help the counselee confess and make restitution when he or she has done something that is wrong according to the spirit of the Scriptures. God has provided these guidelines to free us from the weight of guilt and shame.[7] Confession is how guilt, which depresses self-esteem (see Ps. 38), is removed and relationships are restored, thereby providing affirmation rather than accusation (see Heb. 12:14–15). The counselee needs to remember that one of Satan's most destructive tools is accusation and condemnation (see Rev. 12:10). Failure to confess and forgive self leaves one at the mercy of the condemning False Self. As we confess our sins, the Scripture asserts that the just God forgives us, viewing us through the covering of Christ's blood-atonement (see 1 John 1:9).

3. *Understand the sources of guilt and shame.* The counselee needs to discover the roots of guilt or shame. Frequently, these are dysfunctional thoughts and interactions one has with emotionally significant others (especially parents) who communicate frequent or intense messages of disapproval or rejection. Sometimes the roots are in the teaching and interactions one had with religious authority figures during childhood. Exposure to rigid, gloomy, demanding religious figures who never seem to be satisfied and always point out imperfections is a frequent precursor of guilt and shame in adulthood. As the counselee is able to identify and then evaluate the messages and their sources, he or she is often able to demythologize the deification of those people and the messages with the result of greatly lessened guilt and shame.

4. *Counter rotten rules and faulty filters.* The psychospiritual counselor not only helps the counselee to identify underlying rotten rules (which produce guilt) and faulty filters (which produce shame) but also helps him or her to generate more accurate inner messages.

> *Edward believed, "I can never do anything right," and "I'm stupid." These faulty filters produced intense anger (self-hatred), which led to either irrational acts of violence (punching holes in walls, smashing his windshield) or sexual acting out in the form of cross-dressing and masturbation.*

Initially, I asked Edward to generate counterassertions that were more balanced. Then I asked him to reflect on the assertions and collect any evidence that might show that he needed to alter his original beliefs in line with the counterbeliefs. I also encouraged him to memorize and verbalize the counterbeliefs whenever he began to think and act in the old way.

Gradually, Edward was able to internalize the counter-truths; his anger and acting out (aggression and cross-dressing) progressively lessened until, with the help of other interventions, he achieved high levels of self-control.

One of the major turning points in therapy was when he had cross-dressed and masturbated but was able to report this with the comment, "But somehow I don't feel so deeply shamed by my failure. I feel like I'm making progress. I used to do this several times a week; now I only slip occasionally. I still hate it, but I believe I'm going to overcome it." At this point he had broken the shame —→ acting out —→ intensified shame —→ acting out cycle that had kept him imprisoned since adolescence.

5. *Assess values.* Values are the pillars of one's psychospiritual identity. They provide the framework of motivation, orientation, organization, and commitment for a person's life. We pursue what we value; we guide our behaviors by our most deeply held, central values. We try to live out our values because we believe that they point the way to *shalom.*

In chapter 4 we mentioned the three most prevalent vain values that are promoted by our society as the way to well-being and self-esteem: appearance, achievement, and affluence. Other frequent guiding values are aggrandizement or people pleasing and its opposite, aggression (getting my own way regardless of what happens to others). None of these values provides a stable basis for one's self-esteem; they are all comparative and transient.

The biblical basis of self-esteem is centered on grace rather than on works. It is grounded in the unchanging, eternal love of God toward us. Biblical self-worth is *primarily* focused on what God thinks of us ("Well done, thou good and faithful servant" Matt. 25:21 kjv) rather than on what others think of us (see 1 Sam. 16:7). Biblical self-esteem is rooted in accurate evaluation rather than in self-deflating or self-inflating distortion and social comparison (see Gal. 6:3–4). According to the Scriptures, Christian community is to be a place of affirmation, equality, and countercultural values (see Col. 3:12–17); everyone is gifted and has something to contribute to others. In that sense, each person in the community of believers is an important contributor (see Rom. 12:3–8; 1 Cor. 12:1–31). The Scriptures also affirm that our goal within community is to build each other up into maturity (see Eph. 4:12–13).

6. *Adjust expectations.* Part of the problem with most people who struggle with debilitating guilt or shame is their unrealistic expectations, which produce unhealthy self-perception. Typically, they are perfectionists. The counseling process must help them to adjust the unreachable and irrational demands of significant others that have been internalized as their own expectations. Counselees need to internalize the truth that perfection belongs only to God. Their imperfection, then, is not a failure but a fact of human existence. Their guilt and shame are likely due to false filters that tell them they can always do (be) better. To a certain extent, this is true for all of us. However, the difference for the guilt and shame-filled person is the tone of moral condemnation associated with these failures. For the healthy person, the gap between ideal and real (the way we would like to act or be and the way we are) is an occasion for continuing growth and challenge, rather than an opportunity for self-punishment.

7. *Accept the dark side of themselves.* A surprising number of people within the Christian community are plagued by the anxiety that they will lose control of themselves and either will not be able to stop some horrible thought or will act it out. Generally, these people are sensitive, passive, kind people who want to be good children of God. When the dark side of thoughts appear that are so contradictory to how both they and others see them, they are typically devastated.

> *Gary was horrified, terrified, and guilt-ridden about thoughts of violence and sexual mutilation that suddenly appeared during a time of great transition in his life and uncertainty about a woman he wanted to marry. Part of the process*

of gaining control over his thoughts and feelings involved his coming to grips with the existence of a dark side within him. His entire sense of self and communication to self was "goodness"; he saw himself and was perceived by others as gentle, compassionate, loving, helpful, kind, and Christlike.

As awful as it initially sounded to him, Gary was encouraged to accept and embrace his dark side while affirming that Christ had died for all of him and loved him thoroughly, including the dark side that specifically needed to be redeemed. As he did this and was helped to see that his thoughts were not *his behaviors but that he was in control of his behaviors, he began to recover. Gary also took a small dosage of antianxiety medication for a short while to help break the anxiety cycle.*

8. *Immerse themselves in Scripture.* Part of Gary's recovery involved in-depth immersion in Scripture. This assured him of God's love and ability to redeem the total person, as exemplified by such brutal figures as Saul/Paul, who considered himself the greatest sinner of all, yet redeemed by the Savior (see 1 Tim. 1:15–16). It is particularly helpful to emphasize Scriptures that tell of God's responsiveness and grace toward those who seek Him. Also helpful are Scriptures that assure those who are currently filled with shame that they will have a future of joy (see Isa. 61) and hope (see Jer. 29:11) if they allow God to lead them and love them.

9. *Find and commit themselves to God's special purposes.* Drawing on such passages as Psalm 139, the counselor can help counselees to see that they have unique roles to play in God's plan of the ages. That role, regardless of the particulars of career path, is to live a life of total consecration to the Lord, thereby shining as his light in a particular life context at this point in human history.

10. *Identify their gifts and abilities.* According to the Scriptures, every believer is gifted. Although it is easy for people to start ranking the spiritual gifts and assigning differential status, the Scriptures affirm each gift and each member of the Christian community as equally valuable (see Rom. 12:3–8).

11. *Realize that no one (but God) will ever be totally affirming.* Counselees need to adjust expectations or they will end up

disappointed, disillusioned, and cut off from the love that is there in less than unconditional terms. The truth of the matter is that human love is *not* totally unconditional; even Rogerian therapists are conditional when taken out of their offices! We need to help counselees look for and appreciate love that is given, rather than focus on the absence of perfect love.

12. *Avoid generalizing and exaggerating weaknesses and criticisms.* Just because the counselee has areas to work on does not mean he or she is *all* bad. The counselee may need to fight off perfectionism that typically comes from parents who have very high expectations and are not expressively affirming. The person may need to directly confront areas of weakness and consciously choose to see them as opportunities both for God's grace and for improvement. The counselor should challenge and encourage the counselee to denounce such sweeping generalities as "I'll never be able to do anything right," "I always make mistakes," "Nobody likes the way I am," or "It's no use, I'll never amount to anything."

13. *Avoid comparisons.* This is especially difficult in a status-saturated society, but counselees must set their will against comparing themselves with others. They must be encouraged to evaluate themselves with accuracy and take pride in how God evaluates them (see Gal. 6:3–5). Comparisons lead to feelings of inferiority or superiority, jealousy or pride.

14. *Develop competencies.* Competence builds confidence. Encourage the counselee to develop new work skills, hobbies, and practical skills. Fulfilling the creation mandate to "rule over" (skillfully manage) the created order (Gen. 1:28) by interacting skillfully with one's world increases a person's sense of self-respect and optimism.

15. *Go to Jesus in prayer when they start doubting or defending.* Encourage counselees to tell Christ exactly what they are feeling. It is also helpful to review memorized Scripture in situations that typically create self-doubt.

NOTES

1. Emily Marlin, *Genograms: The New Tool for Exploring the Personality, Career and Love Patterns You Inherit* (New York: Contemporary Books, 1989);

Monica McGoldrick and Randy Gerson, *Genograms in Family Assessment* (New York: Norton, 1985).

2. Steven J. Danish, Anthony R. D'Augelli, and Allen L. Hauer, *Helping Skills: A Basic Training Program, Trainee's Workbook*, 2d ed. (New York: Human Sciences Press, 1980), 40–42.

3. See Craig W. Ellison, ed., *Your Better Self: Christianity, Psychology and Self-Esteem* (San Francisco: Harper and Row, 1983) for a thorough discussion of self-esteem issues.

4. Ronald Potter-Efron and Patricia Potter-Efron, *Letting Go of Shame: Understanding How Shame Affects Your Life* (San Francisco: Harper and Row, 1989), 14. Also refer to Sandra D. Wilson, *Released from Shame: Recovery for Adult Children of Dysfunctional Families* (Downers Grove: InterVarsity, 1990) for a Christian treatment of the shame problem.

5. More extensive therapeutic interventions for guilt and shame may be found in Wilson, *Released from Shame*, 5.

6. S. Bruce Narramore, *No Condemnation* (Grand Rapids: Zondervan, 1985).

7. William G. Justice, Jr., *Guilt and Forgiveness: How God Can Help You Feel Good About Yourself* (Grand Rapids: Baker, 1980).

Chapter Eleven

Relational Well-Being

*Then God said, "Let us make man in our own image,
in our likeness, and let them rule . . . over all the
earth. . . . It is not good for the man to be alone. I will
make a helper suitable for him."*

Genesis 1:26; 2:18

HUMAN BEINGS ARE INESCAPABLY INTERPERSONAL. Adam and Eve
(and all of us since) were created in the image of the triune
God—a relational being. We are conceived through sexual intimacy, are nurtured in a mother's womb, are cared for by
others throughout infancy and childhood, form friendships and
develop partnerships, work with others, marry, and start the
cycle all over again with our own children. Even hermits are
not totally devoid of human relationships—they depend to some
degree on others for certain necessities of life. Most of the joys
and stresses of life come about in the context of relationships.

It is within that context that we learn who we are and how
to feel about ourselves. Relationships trigger our emotions, affect
our motivation, influence our choices, impact our behaviors,
and shape our sense of self. Relationships are the construction
site for values, controlling assumptions, learning, conditioning, and characteristic behavior patterns. They are the molders
of personality.

Relationships may be sources of *shalom* or distress. Frequently they produce a mixture of both. Healthy relationships are significant providers of acceptance, belonging, feelings of competence, equity, identity, security, significance, and transcendence. Negative, distorted, rejecting, conflicted, and imbalanced relationships are major contributors to the stress of life. They create stress by failing to nurture or by wounding our psychospiritual well-being.

In one way or another, broken or distorted relationships create the distress of deepened ontological deficits. The impact is greatest in relationships that are emotionally bonded or valued. Negative feedback from parents about one's characteristics creates unhealthy feelings of self-doubt and low self-esteem that color our perceptions and responses to life in a stress-enhancing way. Distorted relationships create faulty patterns of relating to others that neurotically or psychotically prevent psychospiritual needs from being met. Rejecting relationships lead to significant deficits in all eight areas of psychospiritual need. Furthermore, the devastating pain of rejection usually prompts desperate and faulty ways of trying to cope and find *shalom*. Conflicted relationships, at the very least, prevent positive psychospiritual need fulfillment from the person one is at odds with. The conflict itself is a source of continuing stress.

COMMUNICATION

Do not let any unwholesome talk come out of your mouths, but only what is helpful for building others up according to their needs, that it may benefit those who listen.

Ephesians 4:29

One way of reducing stress and promoting relational well-being is to improve basic communication skills. Human communication, however, is fraught with opportunities for misunderstanding and conflict. This is because we have no way of directly transferring one person's thoughts or feelings to another person. Instead, we must rely on the more indirect process of exchanging symbols through words and nonverbal communication. Even if we could directly transfer thoughts and feelings, there would still be some conflict because of differences in background, values, purposes, commitments, and personality. For example, the same word may have different connotations depending upon the emotional meanings associated with it from one family to another.

Even if people were to use precise dictionary definitions in their discourse with each other, there would be problems. For example, there are more than six hundred thousand words available in the English language. Of these, an educated adult uses about two thousand. The most frequently used words (five hundred) have approximately fourteen thousand different definitions according to standard dictionaries. Some words have up to one hundred or more different meanings!

The communication picture is all the more foggy when we realize that understanding, or shared meaning, is not simply based on words. Rather, approximately 80 percent of the meanings that we make as we communicate are based on nonverbal cues! These are significantly less precise than words and more open to misunderstanding. This is because similar cues may have different (and sometimes opposite) potential meanings, and meanings derived from nonverbal communication depend heavily on the history of the relationship and the current context. We depend so much on nonverbal cues because we realize that people cannot manage and manipulate them as easily as words. The problem is that because of their impreciseness, we can easily misinterpret them.

As a result, it is critically important that those having relational difficulties be evaluated and assisted, as needed, to develop basic communication skills. They need to understand that the possibilities of misunderstanding are significant, given the information we have just discussed. In fact, it is a wonder that human beings *ever* arrive at shared meaning! All interpretations or meanings made from another person's communication should be regarded as tentative. This is especially true of communication that is emotion-laden. When communication is delivered or received with intense, negative emotions, there is an even *greater* possibility of misunderstanding and conflict.

Counselees should be encouraged to carefully scrutinize their interpretations before responding to the other person. This requires that one's emotions be disciplined and held in check. It is easy to fly off the handle if one does not take care to clarify the intentions and meaning of the verbal/nonverbal message. The problem is that the response may be inappropriate to the real meaning of the message and may create unnecessary conflict and division.

Scrutinizing one's interpretations involves developing a habit of saying things such as: "It sounds like you're saying . . ."; "I think I hear you saying . . ."; "Are you saying. . . ?"; "I'm not sure I understand what you're really saying, could you say it again in a different way?" The emphasis is on being tentative and verifying before reacting.

Scrutinizing also gives the other person a second chance to formulate and deliver his or her message. Who among us has not said things in a different way than was intended? All of us have moments, especially when the context is emotionally charged, when we have difficulty putting our thoughts and feelings into the right words and tones.

Conveying empathy is another important communication skill. Empathy is entering into the feelings of the other person in a supportive and positive way. Relationships are built and healed as those involved feel that the other person both understands and cares about them. The use of reflection helps to build empathy. Reflection is the nonjudgmental use of content paraphrasing and identifying the apparent feelings of the other person. Essentially, it is putting one's self into another person's shoes. When we hear another person accurately reflecting back our concerns and picking up on our feelings in a supportive way, we are encouraged and helped. Role-playing with the counselor and specific assignments in real life can help a person acquire this skill.[1]

Counselees should also be encouraged not to send mixed messages as a way of hiding from possible negative reactions. Often poor communication is due to messages that are intentionally vague, indirect, or ambiguous. People usually send these types of messages when they want to deny their true intentions or avoid painful feedback that might come from a more clear or direct message. But healthy communication is assertive.

ASSERTIVENESS

Speaking the truth in love. . . .

Ephesians 4:15

Unfortunately, assertiveness has often received bad press in Christian circles. Properly understood, assertiveness is *not* a selfish, aggressive push for personal rights. It is *not* a demand to get whatever one wants. It is *not* insensitively steamrolling over other people.

Rather, assertiveness appears to be the primary mode of human interaction and communication that God intended. Of the three general ways of relating—assertive, aggressive, and passive—aggression (blaming others) and passivity (hiding) were the automatic responses of fallen Adam and Eve. Prior to that time, Adam and Eve had a direct, positive, nonmanipulative, intimate, and nonpower-oriented relationship with God and with each other.

The interaction style displayed by Jesus Christ was clearly assertive. His way was "full of grace and truth" (John 1: 14). His relationships and communications were rooted in his identity, his calling, his character, his inner commitments, and his values. He did not cower in passivity or crush others with aggression. During his ministry, he assertively chose those whom he wished to socialize with even when they were the wrong kind of people. He assertively rejected Satan's appeals. He chose to minister to people on the Sabbath, not because he was an aggressive rebel but because his principles of conduct were based on divine love. He was not afraid to say what he thought and felt. Even on the cross, the occasion of his self-sacrifice, Jesus asserted himself: he refused the sponge, pardoned the repentant thief, and resisted the temptation to call out legions of angels and take himself off the cross (thereby destroying his mission). He also forgave those who crucified him and instructed John to take care of his mother.

A key phrase from Ephesians 4:15 that describes assertiveness is "speaking the truth in love, we will in all things grow up into him who is the Head, that is Christ." When we are assertive, we *speak* (as compared to passive silence and disallowing thoughts and feelings; or aggressive shouting). We speak the *truth*. In Ephesians this refers to the truth of the Gospel, but I believe we can expand this to mean the truth in general. This includes telling the truth about what one thinks or feels, instead of hiding it. Finally, when we are assertive we speak the truth *in love*. This has to do with the how, when, where, and why of speaking the truth. Assertiveness is interaction and communication that is motivated by respect and concern for the other person as well as for one's self.[2]

Assertive people are *proactive*. That is, they anticipate, strategize, and constructively act upon their world out of inner principles, purposes, priorities, and the particular situation. They are not reactive. They do not respond to emotionally charged situations either by withdrawing and repressing (passivity) or by attacking and intimidating. They face issues and initiate action that is not primarily designed to protect themselves from pain. They are not people pleasers who cave in to the pressures of others. Out of a base of faith and courage they take reasonable risks.

Assertive people are *partner-based* rather than power-based. Their relationships are horizontal, between emotional equals or adults. They do not seek out or accept the role of child or superior parent in their adult relationships. Consequently, they are focused on building one another up into the mature and whole persons God has intended. Their interactions are marked by mutual respect rather than by criticism, blaming, shaming, and controlling (aggressiveness) or by dependency, domination, and diminishment of self (passivity).

Unlike passive people, who have difficulty making decisions and want to be told what to do, or aggressive people, who are ready to make others' decisions for them, those who are assertive emphasize dialogue and joint decision-making (if appropriate).

They neither control others nor are controlled by others; rather, their focus is on self-control under God's control. They are neither people pleasers, who will take care of everyone but themselves, nor people pushers, who bully others physically, emotionally, or spiritually. Finally, when a person is consistently assertive, he or she is interdependent, maintaining a healthy balance between identity/individuality and intimacy, being neither dependent nor codependent, emotionally enmeshed with others, or alienated from close relationships in an overemphasis on separateness.

Because of the fallen world that we live in, no one is naturally or completely assertive. However, if raised in a home marked by consistent assertiveness, a child will find it easier to be consistently assertive as an adult. Regardless, assertiveness is a set of attitudes and skills that can be learned.

People being trained in assertiveness first need to identify any faulty familial messages or rotten rules that have promoted nonassertiveness and would likely interfere with becoming assertive.

> **Lana,** a thirty-two-year old single woman, had difficulty forming and maintaining relationships with men, was deeply angry toward her mother, and was highly codependent in her relationships. She had learned a number of family rules that kept her imprisoned in passivity. Among those rotten rules (rotten because they produced distress rather than shalom, over time) were: "Take care of others." "Taking care of yourself is selfish." "Don't rock the boat." "Your family comes first (before your own needs and wishes)." "Make others happy." "Don't express negative feelings." "Don't be weak and vulnerable." "Always be happy." "Never air dirty laundry."

During the course of the training, messages like these should be discussed thoroughly as hindrances to healthy assertiveness.

Counselees should be encouraged to verbalize how the faulty filters and rotten rules might interfere with assertiveness and with *shalom*. They need to understand that these messages have intense, psychomoral force—the filters and rules have been internalized as yardsticks of whether they are good or bad people. Consequently, attempts to change these internal beliefs and rules with new assertive choices may produce some initial anxiety or guilt as they are violated by the counselee's new assertive choices. Counselees should be informed, however, that as they consistently make assertive choices they will quickly begin to feel a growing sense of self-respect and peace inside because they are now choosing to act in the way God originally intended.

Once counselees understand the three styles of interaction, they should be encouraged to make at least one assertive response daily and to log it. Initially, the choices should not relate to the *most* risky and difficult areas of their life but should relate to people and areas of life in which they are typically not assertive. Through extensive role-play of assertiveness in the areas of greatest difficulty, counselees will gradually choose to be assertive in those areas as well. The primary reasons for logging daily assertive choices is to keep assertiveness flooding their awareness as they learn new ways of thinking and interacting. This also provides a growth record that will encourage them as they look back on their progress over time.

CONFLICT RESOLUTION

Live in harmony with one another. . . . Do not be conceited. Do not repay anyone evil for evil. Be careful to do what is right in the eyes of everybody. If it is possible, as far as it depends on you, live at peace with everyone.

Romans 12:16–18

First go and be reconciled to your brother; then come and offer your gift.

Matthew 5:24

Conflict may arise as a result of different goals, different ways of pursuing goals, clashing values, misunderstood communication, perceived violation of a person's rules for relationship, insults or put-downs, betrayal of trust, contests of power or wills, or opposition to personal requests. Unresolved conflict typically produces continuing stress because of a variety of possible feelings including anger, bitterness, damaged self-esteem, grief, revenge, regret, and victimization. Conflict can be positive if it is constructively resolved because it can lead to reevaluation of positions and creative compromise. Conflict can also breathe fresh air into a stagnant relationship, encourage thorough and honest communication and better understanding, and produce individual and interpersonal growth.

Conflict resolution is promoted by assertiveness. As conflicting parties focus on the problem, rather than on self- or other-blaming, they are able to be more objective. In constructive conflict-resolution each person exercises the self-discipline of saying *no* to kitchen-sinking. That is, they must refuse the temptation to drag in other issues, past offenses, comments about the other person's flaws, references to the other person's family of origin, etc. The focus must be on the current conflict. As each person respectfully expresses his or her thoughts and feelings and the other parties listen with respect, the conflict is more likely to be resolved with an aftermath of good feeling and strengthened relationship.

Assertiveness means to approach the conflict this way: "We have a problem. Let's work on it together and try to find a solution." It is based on honest expression of positions and feelings. Assertive problem-solving means to look for and accept negotiation and compromise; it is recognizing that each person will likely have to give so that both persons will be treated fairly. Constructive conflict resolution emphasizes good listening. Instead of interrupting the other person or hearing certain buzz words and turning the other person off in order to make up a good defensive reply, the assertive person tries to hear the feelings and unspoken messages behind the other person's position. This kind of listening reduces defensiveness, creates an atmosphere of caring, and helps to communicate respect and the desire to reach a fair resolution.

Constructive conflict resolution also requires both the willingness to forgive and the willingness to ask forgiveness. If a person holds onto perceived hurts and seeks retribution, there will be little success in resolving conflict because that will stimulate a vicious cycle of defensiveness and counter-retribution. If a person refuses to admit the wrongs or hurts committed, the other party will feel that person is unfair, insensitive, and unteachable. If that is the case, the "victim" will be less likely to take the risks necessary to soften his or her position and adopt a posture of compromise and negotiation. After all, if only one person compromises and negotiates, it is surrender— not constructive resolution.

Constructive conflict resolution begins with assessment:

Is there a conflict?

Who is affected by this conflict?

What are the issues involved?

Why is this a conflict?

Are there underlying issues that are not obvious but are actually the source of the conflict?

What are the consequences of not resolving this conflict?

What are the results of resolving it constructively?

The counselee should think through these questions and write down responses in order to formulate the conflict in terms of a problem to be objectively solved.

> One young family was in total uproar over the refusal of their son, **Kyle**, to complete his homework. His work habits reminded his mother, Ilsa, of her father, who was despised by her mother for having no ambition and not following through. Ilsa's intense anger toward the son drew the husband, John, into the conflict and they ended up fighting with each other while the son played computer games.
>
> After thorough discussion, the couple (with my help) formulated the conflict as a problem to be solved: How can we get Kyle to do his homework consistently, without Ilsa becoming upset and angry? Further discussion helped them to realize that their approach to that point had been negative—they had tried to motivate Kyle by threats, yelling, and punishment. They agreed that their approach had not worked.

After formulating the conflict into a problem, I encouraged John and Ilsa to brainstorm possible ways to positively motivate Kyle. This meant that Ilsa would have to back off and control her perfectionism and anger. They proposed several possible solutions, threw out any that either one of them was totally uncomfortable with, rated each possible solution that remained on a scale of one to ten as to probable effectiveness, combined their scores, and then discussed the pros and cons of their first three choices. They were encouraged to listen carefully and respectfully to their partner's point of view.

Their first choice was to make a chart and put it on the refrigerator. The chart listed each subject Kyle was taking. When he had completed all of his homework for that subject for the night, he was allowed to initial that spot on the chart. When he reached a certain level of completion for the week, he was to be given a small reward. Also, his parents were to explicitly express praise for homework completed. At the end of a month, if he reached a certain criteria, he was to be allowed to choose a larger reward. Initially, Ilsa felt he should not get a reward unless he did 100 percent of his homework for the week. After discussion the parents agreed that they could live with an 85 percent criteria, because that was a lot better than 0 percent.

Finally, an experimental or test period should be agreed upon, to try out the proposed solutions. At the end of the test period (a month is usually a good time frame), the solutions should be mutually reevaluated: How well are they working? Does something need to be altered? What, and how? If revisions are made, another test period should be agreed on.

John and Ilsa agreed to allow four weeks for their experiment. Although there were some relapses in the first two weeks, the results were almost immediate. After one month, they concluded that not only was the plan working and Kyle was getting his homework completed, but that the anger, conflict, and chaos in the home were greatly reduced. By the end of the quarter, Kyle was getting A's in his classes and received a special letter of commendation from his principal.

It is important that people in conflict allow sufficient time for the conflict to be thoroughly discussed. Rushed comments as a spouse exits for work generally make things worse. It is usually helpful to set a definite time and to allow a minimum of an hour for discussion and resolution. Although this may seem like a long time, most conflicts (especially in marriages) end up consuming much greater amounts of time and energy if they are not resolved properly.

> *Andrew refused to discuss his anger over a decision Linda had made about the house. Instead, he had not spoken to her at all for seven months when she contacted my office!*

While that is extreme, it is not unusual for unresolved conflicts to upset marital and family relationships for two to three days when they could likely be resolved in one to two hours.

If people are unable to reach agreement on an issue, they need to problem-solve how they will constructively live with their differences so that a climate of pressuring or punishment is not established.

FORGIVENESS

> *Therefore, as God's chosen people, holy and dearly loved, clothe yourselves with compassion, kindness, humility, gentleness and patience. Bear with each other and forgive whatever grievances you may have against one another. Forgive as the Lord forgave you. And over all these virtues put on love, which binds them together in perfect unity.*

> Colossians 3:12–14

As we have already mentioned, asking for and granting forgiveness are two critical ingredients in healing relationships and troubled emotions. Someone has rightly said, "A good marriage is a union of two good forgivers."

Confession of wrongs or hurts committed heals relationships by altering the victim's perception that the other person is insensitive, unfair, and does not care about him or her. The only alternatives to this are denial or blaming—neither of which encourages trust and love. Rather, these defensive approaches result in the victim feeling both wronged and unloved. He or she is likely to feel unsafe in the relationship, if not bitter and vindictive, as attempts are made to establish the truth being denied by the other person.

It is important for men in particular to realize that a wrong is not just an objective injustice but may involve actions or words that are unloving and unkind. Saying or doing things that promote (deepen) existential deficits and damage another person's self-worth are wrongs that need to be confessed. Wounding another person psychospiritually is just as much an offense as wounding someone physically. At the same time, it is important that neither partner wear their feelings on their sleeve (be hypersensitive) as a way of manipulating or controlling the relationship. In a mature and healthy relationship, those involved are concerned about building each other up and ministering to each other compassionately and sensitively so that psychospiritual needs are met in a relational context of love.

Asking forgiveness requires honesty and humility. It should be practiced by parents with their children as well as between adults. Parents are not perfect, and older children know that. Asking a child's forgiveness is important for the child to be able to trust the parents and to be able to draw close to them, knowing that they will try to treat the child fairly and with care. It also teaches children that asking forgiveness is a natural and good thing, rather than teaching them denial and blaming.

Granting forgiveness is equally essential for healing and healthy relationships. The major difficulty is that all of us have enough sense of justice that we want wrongs against us to be properly and promptly punished. Of course, we are often likely to excuse similar offenses that we commit as due to justifying circumstances, having a bad day, etc. These tendencies reflect our innate sense of equity that has been twisted by the Fall. At any rate, we want injustice dealt with and wrongs punished, especially if the other person refuses to confess his or her wrongdoing and does not show proper contrition.

One way of seeing that justice is conducted is to hand down

to the offender a life sentence of anger and rejection. The problem is that in order for the offender to be punished in this way, the victim has to continue to be involved, dispensing the punishment by refusing to allow the relationship to be healed. This not only keeps the relationship broken but keeps the victim fixated on the wrongs of the past, marinating in hurt feelings and bitterness.

When a person has refused to grant forgiveness to someone for a long time, another destructive thing occurs. Part of the victim's basic identity *becomes* victim. That is, the person's very sense of self is filled with old wounds. The person's emotional life is governed by the hurt that is stored and treasured inside. As long as forgiveness is withheld, *the identity of the individual* is centrally defined by the past offenses. Caught in the past, the victim is unable to keep growing. This creates a problem for many because to let go of the grievance and forgive, means to feel as though they are giving up their very self, which has been structured by their hurts. They feel they will be totally vulnerable, without a sense of inner strength and defense. In a sense, by defining themselves as victim, they fear that they will become worse victims if they give up their victim role. They are afraid that if they forgive, the person will take advantage of them and hurt them again. It is important for these counselees to understand that by identifying themselves as victim, they have adopted a passive view of themselves. They need to learn assertive self-perspectives and skills hand-in-hand with the process of granting forgiveness.

Many people struggle with forgiving and forgetting. They find that feelings of hurt and bitterness reemerge when they thought they had forgiven. The reason that the hurts resurface is that the conscious and rational act of forgiving generally does not instantly and totally change their emotionally based victim identity, which feeds on self-pity. This is not really an issue of forgetting but of *reaffirming* the forgiveness they have already granted. Each reaffirmation helps them to further reconstruct their identity around a healthy, victim-free identity instead of the self-pitying victim identity they previously nurtured.

It is helpful for many to consider the possibility that the

offender's actions were not intentional and therefore not meant to be harmful and malicious. The offender, consequently, may not see any need to ask forgiveness. The offender's actions may also be the result of destructive and dysfunctional patterns learned during the person's developmental years from parents, and perhaps even passed down for several generations ("He punishes the children and their children for the sin of the fathers to the third and fourth generations," Exod. 34:7). While recognizing these patterns is helpful, they may be so deeply ingrained that it is extremely difficult for the person to change.

The counselee may also need to consider carefully whether the sense of being offended is due to these other factors:

1. Rotten family-of-origin rules that are not shared by other people. Perhaps, for example, the offender does not operate by the rule that the primary responsibility of one's life is to do whatever is necessary to make the spouse feel happy. At this point the victim may need help in recognizing and releasing dysfunctional rules rather than granting forgiveness to the supposed offender.

2. The manipulative use of perceived offenses is a way of exercising psychomoral control and power in the relationship. If one can see the other as an offender, the victim has a power advantage.

3. One's own coping mechanisms are imposed on the other person. For example, perfectionism (which is designed to minimize pain by insisting that everything be done the right way) may result in feelings of being hurt by the lack of sensitivity and carelessness of one's partner. In actuality, it may be simply that the nonperfectionist is functioning in a healthy manner, not having bought into the dysfunctional pattern of trying to control possible chaos and pain.

Certainly, granting forgiveness is greatly assisted as a believer focuses on the example and forgiving work of Jesus Christ on the cross. Counselees may find it easier to forgive if they can see that, in God's eyes, *everyone* has committed hideous offenses (sins) that are a horrible stench to God's nostrils, and yet God has forgiven *us*. By reminding counselees that Jesus, the holy and righteous judge, will perfectly execute justice toward all, including them, and has clearly commanded that they are not to seek justice (revenge) because God will vindicate (see Rom. 12:17–21), the counselor will help them let go of the need to punish.

The goal, both of asking and granting forgiveness, is to be freed from the fixation of victimization and to restore a broken relationship to health so that each person can lovingly nourish the other's psychospiritual needs and experience *shalom*. It is virtually impossible for human beings to consistently experience *shalom* if their lives are marred by broken and distorted relationships.

BUILDING INTIMACY

> *If you have any encouragement from being united with Christ, if any comfort from his love, if any fellowship with the Spirit, if any tenderness and compassion, then make my joy complete by being like-minded, having the same love, being one in spirit and purpose.*

Philippians 2:1

Love is the fundamental building block of *shalom*. We were created by a loving God for the purpose of companionship with him. God recognized Adam's need for relationship with another being who was compatible with him, so he took Eve from Adam's side.

We were made to love and to be loved. If we were to be completely, consistently, and perfectly loved, our psychospiritual needs would be met to a large degree, and we would not have nearly the levels of distress and pain that we currently encounter. The reason, of course, is not that God stopped loving human beings but that human beings have become defensive and unable to receive his love. In our fallen condition we are also unable to perfectly love one another. The result is at least some level of pain in our relationships. The power of love to produce *shalom*, however, makes it essential that we *learn* how to build intimacy to the highest degree possible.

Intimacy does not just happen. It requires a continuing, long-term commitment between people. Intimacy is having a sense of being cared for, a feeling of closeness, a perception of unity, an experience of mutual understanding, a sense of togetherness. It is a celebration of companionship and communion.

Building intimacy is a gradual movement from sharing superficialities to sharing self and secrets as the result of trust. Intimacy is a process that is dynamic. It has an ebb and flow to it; in any relationship there are cycles of closeness and distance.

There are three basic kinds of intimacy: spiritual (spirit), emotional (soul), and sexual (body). Spiritual intimacy involves the sharing of a fundamental orientation to life and relationship with God. Emotional intimacy is the sharing of common values, dreams, goals, and experiences in a climate of caring, concern, and closeness. Sexual intimacy builds on the other two if it is to reach its fullest expression, as husband and wife physically unite in love.

As we share intimately with another, we feel a deep sense of peace, inner joy, and well-being (*shalom*). Intimacy inspires us with purpose, infuses us with motivation, and energizes us with optimism. Without positive intimacy, we seek for ways to assure ourselves that we count: we compete, we overachieve, we run over others to get to the top. But those paths bring stress rather than *shalom*. Or, we despair and give up, feeling as though we do not matter at all if we do not matter to someone.

Faith is the foundation stone of intimacy. Faith in God empowers us to love another (remain committed and desire the best) through difficulties, to care when naturally speaking we could care less, to remain faithful when it seems foolish, to hope when things appear hopeless. Faith in the character, intentions, and potential of our partner is also essential. This includes thinking good when it would be easier to think evil, giving the benefit of the doubt when we doubt, seeing the potential for growth, and encouraging one's partner through his or her anxieties and fears. Faith is commitment to the promise that there can and will be a future for the relationship. As we are able to see that every disruption of life and relationship is a spiritual opportunity to see that God is there to help and grant the power to love, our ability to build and maintain intimacy is strengthened immensely.

Drawing close to God individually and sharing together spiritually are key elements of growing intimacy. As we draw close to God we are empowered to love, forbear, forgive, communicate graciously, build each other up, and display the fruit of the Spirit (see Gal. 5:22–23). We are also enabled to exercise greater self-control over developmental distortions, ego defenses, and temptations that produce turmoil and trouble within close relationships. Intimacy with God also means that he will meet our *deepest* needs for love and acceptance. When at times our partner fails to meet our needs, we are better able to remain secure in God and to forgive. Drawing from our relationship with God means that we are also in a better position to give to our partner, instead of draining him or her to meet our own needs.

Other building blocks of intimacy include cultivating caring, sharing mutual experiences, respecting differences, listening well, and building each other up.

Caring is the ability to sense spoken and unspoken needs of our partner, and to respond in ways that communicate "I love you," "I want the best for you." It is not so much problem-solving as it is coming alongside, letting our companion express his or her feelings, and giving him or her the assurance that we will not abandon.

In marriages, particularly, this requires our understanding that we each have a different language of love.[3] This means that we have each learned ways of speaking, touching, or doing that communicate "I love you," that make us feel loved. Husbands and wives should be encouraged to write out a language of love list that tells their partner, "When you _____, I feel loved (cherished, valued, wanted, cared for) and want to remain in this relationship." It would be helpful for the couple to generate an initial list of ten to twelve items that are positively worded, specific, and repeatable.

It is best for the couple to develop the list privately and then to review it with the counselor to make sure the criteria (positive, specific, repeatable) are met and there are no hidden zingers. After revising the list and reminding the couple that this is *not* a list of demands but a way of communicating what will make them feel loved, the couple should exchange lists and be challenged to implement at least one per day, *regardless of what the partner does.* When a person is aware that his or her partner has implemented an expression of love language, that communication should be explicitly acknowledged and affirmed verbally to the partner.

Caring can be shown especially at times of crisis. Crises give us an opportunity to draw together or fall apart. If we stand with our friend who is hurting, intimacy will be strengthened.

Intimacy is a movement from *I* to *we*, which is encouraged as two share life together in various ways. Three kinds of *we* experiences that build intimacy are: praying together, planning together, and playing together. As we communicate honestly and deeply with God, we reveal a personal and vulnerable side of ourselves to another person, which allows us to be known and to be drawn together in spirit-oneness. As we plan and make decisions together in a climate of respect, we become a team rather than separate entities. Sharing life goals and setting priorities together promotes a sense of true partnership. Playing together builds intimacy because it provides for high-reward (*shalom*)/low-cost (pain) interaction with one another. In the context of a committed, ongoing relationship, it provides positive relief from the struggles, stresses, and strains that so easily fill daily life. Playing requires discipline (of time) because it is often looked at as a frill. Counselors often find it helpful for couples to schedule pray and play time into their calendars on a regular basis or these times will never happen.

Respecting differences is critical for building intimacy. We tend to want others to be like us because this provides a kind of security. Differences can be threatening because they challenge us with ways of thinking, feeling, and acting that are not like *our* ways of thinking, feeling, and acting. They create anxiety deep inside of us that perhaps our way of being is not right, or is inferior. However, if we do not accept differences we will not enjoy intimacy, because no two people are exactly alike.

None of us likes to feel rejected for who we are and how we do things, or to feel as though we are someone else's rehabilitation project. That is why I encourage couples to be sure that they are completely comfortable with who their fiancee is right now, and not to marry with the idea that one of them will be able to change the other.

Building each other up is based upon accentuating the positives. Partners need to maximize affirmation and minimize criticism of each other if they are to experience consistent intimacy. Maximizing affirmation includes focusing on the positives, being courteous, expressing explicit appreciation (especially for the routine things that a partner does to show loving concern and to make life easier), and showing interest in each other's life and interests. Minimizing criticism includes being assertive, making molehills out of mountains, verbalizing feelings (talk, don't act out), and relating to each other on an adult-to-adult level (rather than parent-child).

NOTES

1. Exercises such as those found in Gerard Egan, *Exercises in Helping Skills*, 4th ed. (Pacific Grove, Calif.: Brooks-Cole, 1990); and James J. Messina, *Tools for Communications* and *Tools for Relationships* (Tampa, Fl.: Advanced Development Systems, 1989) are helpful.

2. This material first appeared in slightly different form in Craig W. Ellison and Edward S. Maynard, *Healing for the City: Counseling in the Urban Setting* (Grand Rapids: Zondervan, 1992), 191–93.

3. See Judson Swihart, *How Do You Say I Love You?* (Downers Grove: InterVarsity, 1977).

Chapter Twelve

Spiritual Well-Being

*But the fruit of the Spirit is love, joy, peace, patience,
kindness, goodness, faithfulness, gentleness and self-
control. Against such things there is no law.*

Galatians 5:22–23

SPIRITUAL WELL-BEING IS PRIMARILY THE RESULT of a positive relationship with God that grounds a person in the knowledge and
experience of his love. As the result of a satisfying, personal
relationship with God, a foundation of abiding acceptance,
love, adequacy, respect, identity, security, and significance is
established in one's being. As one's relationship with God
deepens, a sense of vocation or calling also emerges. This normally leads to commitment to purposes that produce ultimate
meaning in life. Commitment to God promotes a sense of purpose that both permeates and transcends the mundane and
temporal. As human beings reach beyond egocentricity to the
eternal, they discover that their need for transcendence is addressed.

Spiritual well-being, as an expression of *shalom*, is not strictly
a spiritual matter. It is interactive with the whole person. One's
relationship with God and ultimate meaning not only are influenced by other people and life's events but influence the

way that we perceive and process life experience. As we have mentioned in earlier chapters, we are truly integrative systems.

In an earlier article, I wrote that:

> It is the *spirit* of human beings which enables and motivates us to search for meaning and purpose in life, to seek the supernatural or some meaning which transcends us, to wonder about our origins and our identities, to require morality and equity. It is the spirit which synthesizes the total personality and provides some sense of energizing direction and order. The spiritual dimension does not exist in isolation from our *psyche* and *soma*, but provides an integrative force.[1]

It is likely that spiritual well-being is not the same thing as spiritual health, but is a reflection of it—much like one's pulse rate or color of complexion are indicators of underlying health. The measurement of spiritual well-being is, then, comparable to a stethoscope rather than to the heart. This conception frees us from the burden of trying to empirically and comprehensively measure the inner contours of our spirit—an impossible task because the spirit is not empirical in nature and has meanings too rich to completely capture through a scientific measure. Instead, measures of spiritual well-being may be seen as general indicators and helpful approximations of the underlying spiritual state.

Spiritual well-being and spiritual maturity are probably not the same either. That is, while spiritual maturity (*teleios*) may produce spiritual well-being, a person who is not particularly mature may experience spiritual well-being. A newborn Christian, for example, is not spiritually mature but may have a very high level of spiritual well-being.

SPIRITUAL WELL-BEING RESEARCH

Research into the nature and experience of spiritual well-being consistently supports this biblical, holistic view. The greatest body of psychospiritual research dealing with these issues to date has been with the Spiritual Well-Being Scale[2] (see appendix 2).

The Spiritual Well-Being Scale provides a general measure of spiritual well-being. Ten of the items were designed to assess a person's religious well-being (satisfaction with one's relationship with God), and ten items measure existential well-being (life purpose and satisfaction). The scale requires approximately ten minutes for completion.

The Spiritual Well-Being Scale (SWBS) is currently being used in a wide variety of research and clinical settings. These include university hospitals, nursing schools, schools of social work, psychology clinics, churches, and various dissertation and thesis projects. Altogether, over 350 studies have been done with the scale since 1976.[3]

The integrative or holistic nature of spiritual well-being has been demonstrated through extensive research with the SWBS.[4] Spiritual well-being is positively related to self-ratings of health,[5] overall adjustment to hemodialysis,[6] hope in female cancer[7] and male AIDS[8] patients, and hardiness among AIDS patients.[9] Those with higher levels of spiritual well-being have lower blood pressure. Cancer patients with higher spiritual well-being have less pain and degree of impairment,[10] less anxiety,[11] social isolation, and despair.[12] People who are chronically ill with diabetes, emphysema, hypertension, or heart failure have less hopelessness about their condition if they have higher spiritual well-being.[13] Both healthy and chronically ill patients are more lonely if their spiritual well-being is low.[14]

With regard to emotional (psychological) well-being, research has found that those higher on spiritual well-being are motivated by a guiding force, characteristic of self-actualization.[15] They also have greater internal locus of control (see their choices as having an effect on what happens in their lives),[16] greater self-esteem,[17] and more hope.[18] Depression,[19] stress,[20] psychopathology,[21] aggressiveness, and conflict avoidance[22] are greater among those with lower levels of spiritual well-being.

Those with greater spiritual well-being are more generally assertive, self-confident, affirming, and able to ask for help. On the other hand, they are less aggressive, dependent, passive, and active avoiders of conflict.[23].

Finally, born-again Christians have higher levels of spiritual well-being than ethical Christians or non-Christians.[24]

Spiritual well-being is positively correlated with the religiosity scale on the MMPI,[25] religiosity as measured on the Buberian religiosity scale,[26] the Intrinsic Religiosity Scale of the Allport and Ross Religious Orientation Survey,[27] and spiritual maturity.[28] Those who see religion as important in their lives,[29] believe in God as a causal agent in life,[30] more frequently attend church,[31] or more frequently have family and personal devotions[32] typically have higher spiritual well-being.

In summary, research results support the conceptualization that spiritual well-being is an interactive product of the meeting of physical, psychological, and relational needs. As the psychospiritual needs of a person are met, the spiritual well-being is increased and vice versa.

THE ROOTS OF TRANSCENDENCE

Although spiritual well-being is the result of the entire human system functioning in a balanced and harmonious way, it is especially interactive with transcendence. This is clearly implied with the two-dimensional conceptualization of the Spiritual Well-Being Scale: religious and existential well-being. Transcendence refers to a sense of ultimate meaning for one's life that stems from one's relationship with God. It is the ability to discover and experience patterns of life-meaning that go beyond the purely natural and to connect with God.

Transcendence is a direct reflection of the character and purposes of God. Human beings find their greatest levels of *shalom* as they stretch toward ultimate purpose and meaning in life that goes beyond just eating, drinking, sex, and menial tasks. *We experience our highest levels of well-being when we have a sense of purpose that is rooted in divine relationship and vocation.*

As we have already suggested in chapter 1, the biblical use of the word *shalom* refers to the absence of strife, conflict, and disharmony. It refers to a peace that comes from wholeness and completeness. It is rooted in a harmonious relationship with God, who is named *Jehovah-Shalom*, through the reconciliation made possible by Jesus Christ.

> Since we have now been justified by his blood,
> how much more shall we be saved from God's wrath

through him! For if, when we were God's enemies, we were reconciled to him through the death of his Son, how much more, having been reconciled shall we be saved through his life! Not only is this so, but we also rejoice in God through our Lord Jesus Christ, through whom we have now received reconciliation.

Romans 5:9–11

For God was pleased to have all his fullness dwell in him, and through him to reconcile to himself all things, whether things on earth or things in heaven, by making peace through his blood, shed on the cross. Once you were alienated from God and were enemies in your minds because of your evil behavior. But now he has reconciled you by Christ's physical body through death to present you holy in his sight, without blemish and free from accusation.

Colossians 1:19–22

The reconciliation made possible through the bridging atonement of Jesus Christ begins in restoring the right relationship with God that was originally intended but has been broken by sin (choosing to live in ways contrary to God's design). There is deep rejoicing in the spirit and soul of the person who has been reconciled to *Jehovah-Shalom*. Several times in the New Testament God is called the God of peace[33] (e.g., Rom. 15:33; 16:20; 2 Cor. 13:11; Phil. 4:9; 1 Thess. 5:23; Heb. 13:20). Jesus the Messiah is referred to as the Prince of Peace (see Isa. 9:6) and as the one who gives peace to us (see John 14:27; 16:33). According to the Bible, God keeps those in perfect peace who trust in him and whose minds are stayed on him (see Isa. 26:3). *Jehovah-Shalom* is the giver of peace. As we do our part of trusting, guarding our imagination (mind), and expressing our needs and anxieties to God in prayer with thanksgiving, the Bible promises that his peace will sustain us (see Phil. 4:6–7). Indeed, Psalm 35:27 tells us that the Lord "delights in the well-being of his servant."

God is not only *Jehovah-Shalom* though. He is also *El Olam*, the everlasting God. "The secret of unfailing strength . . . is unbroken communion with God. Whether in the enthusiasm and vitality of youth, or the waning strength of old age, *El Olam* remains unchanged and unchanging. He is sufficient for old age and every age."[34]

"Do you not know?
    Have you not heard?
The LORD is the everlasting God [*El Olam*],
    the Creator of the ends of the earth.
He will not grow tired or weary
    and his understanding no one can fathom.
He gives strength to the weary
    and increases the power of the weak. . . .
but those who hope in the LORD
    will renew their strength.
They will soar on wings like eagles;
    they will run and not grow weary,
they will walk and not be faint."

                                          Isaiah 40:28–29, 31.

God is also *El Roi*, the God who sees. He sees sin, but he also sees suffering and sorrow. Because of his eternal, overarching perspective, he is able to guide: "I will instruct you and teach you in the way you should go; I will counsel you and *watch over* you" (Ps. 32:8; emphasis added).

God is *Jehovah-Rapha*, the Lord who heals. He is not only the healer of the body, as demonstrated in many of the miracles of Christ, but he is also the healer of the soul (see Ps. 41:4; 147:3; Jer. 3:22). While he is able to heal, however, he does not always choose to do so in a direct way. Sometimes he works at a deeper level of grace that promotes maturity while not removing the difficulty. Paul experienced this: "But he said to me, 'My grace is sufficient for you, for my power is made perfect in weakness'" (2 Cor. 12:9).

As we draw close to God and put into practice the commandments and guidelines that he gives for living life the way he intended, we discover that well-being is further promoted by being reconciled with others *and* by overcoming double-mindedness and internal division.

> For he himself is our peace, who has made the two one and has destroyed the barrier, the dividing wall of hostility. . . . His purpose was to create in himself one new man out of the two, thus making peace, and in this one body to reconcile both of them to God through the cross, by which he put to death their hostility. He came and preached peace to you who were far away and peace to those who were near.
>
> Ephesians 2:14, 15–17.

> For you were once darkness but now you are light in the Lord. Live as children of light (for the fruit of light consists in all goodness, righteousness and truth) and find out what pleases the Lord. Have nothing to do with the fruitless deeds of darkness, but rather expose them. . . . Be very careful, then, how you live—not as unwise but as wise, making the most of every opportunity, because the days are evil. Therefore do not be foolish, but understand what the Lord's will is . . . be filled with the Spirit . . . [then you will be able to] sing and make music in your heart to the Lord.
>
> Ephesians 5:8–11, 15–19.

Spiritual well-being is also rooted in the transcendence of ultimate meaning or purpose that comes from a sense of divinely ordained vocation.

> For we are God's workmanship, created in Christ Jesus to do good works, which God prepared in advance for us to do. ·
>
> Ephesians 2:10

And whatever you do, whether in word or deed,
do it all in the name of the Lord Jesus, giving thanks
to God the Father through him. . . . Whatever you
do, work at it with all your heart, as working for the
Lord, not for men.

Colossians 3:17, 23.

The person who is committed to a personal relationship with
Jehovah-Shalom through the reconciling work of Yeshua is given
the opportunity to experience transcendence as he or she lives
out the kingdom of God on earth. As we work out God's purposes, we find the most satisfying and deep levels of spiritual
well-being. Discovering and living out his purposes grants to
us ultimate meaning that transcends the temporal, the transient, and the trivial.

Do not conform any longer to the pattern of this
world, but be transformed by the renewing of your
mind. Then you will be able to test and approve
what God's will is—his good, pleasing and perfect
will.

Romans 12:2

The world and its desires pass away, but the man
who does the will of God lives forever.

1 John 2:17

Discipleship and stewardship are part of vocation.[35] Vocation is a life-long process of discovering who we are and are
meant to be as children of God. Realizing our calling is essential for a clear sense of identity, maturity, and transcendence.
Vocation involves discovering the purposes of God for me as a
unique person and as a child of God. It also involves my
participation in the shaping of my calling as I step out in faith-
response to the whisperings, nudgings, and invisible leading

of God. Leaps of faith or risk-taking are an essential part of discovering who we are meant to be and how we are to work that out. Indeed, we are to "continue to work out [our] salvation with fear and trembling, for it is God who works in [us] to will and to act according to his good purpose" (Phil. 2:12–13).

Over time, gradually, as we are faithful to our moment-by-moment sense of vocation and are obedient to God's guidelines for Upward Path living, we begin to catch glimpses of the person God wants us to become. As we choose and shape our lives according to this unfolding revelation, we find ourselves maturing in a healthy and holy way. We also experience deep levels of joy (*shalom*).

COMMUNITY

The Christian community is a vital part of the whole process of maturation because it is meant to be a place of guidance, accountability, affirmation, healing, and shared joy that nurtures maturity and *shalom*. It is important that clients be encouraged to participate regularly in churches that function as true communities of believers.

This suggests, of course, that there are evangelical churches that do not function as true communities. Those churches are so focused on institutional forms and other externals that they are not able to be places of genuine nurturing. They are primarily programmatic and impersonal rather than person-focused and caring.

Within a caring Christian community there will be guidance that comes from more formal channels of preaching and teaching. But there will also be individually administered opportunities for guidance through counseling, mentoring, and small-group discipleship. It is vital that these modes of guidance begin with people as they are and not try to squeeze individuals into preshaped molds. An important part of growth toward maturity and *shalom* is accountability (see chapter 8, pages 110–11). Counseling, mentoring (one-to-one discipleship), and even small groups that are drawn together for the purpose of accountability or for specific Downward Path struggles, provide crucial sources for accountability.

It is within genuine Christian community that affirmation, healing, and shared joy occur as well. In this kind of community, people are valued for who they are rather than for what they own or do. Efforts are made to express regular appreciation for each person's vocation and God-given gifts through such means as notes of encouragement, verbal appreciation expressed in Sunday school or other small groups, and even a time of spiritual commissioning for people who have similar senses of vocation (e.g. housewives, business owners, teachers), recognizing that their life situations are opportunities to redemptively work out their salvation and calling.

Healing is recognized in a caring community as a needed and vital part of growing maturity and well-being. Instead of pretending that everyone is perfect, the leadership grants permission for people to be real. They give opportunities for expressing needs and for healing intervention. This may be done in small (self-help) groups, through the ministry of pastor and elders, through the provision of psychospiritual counseling, and through traditional means of prayer support. The message must be communicated that everyone is wounded to some degree and that we need not endeavor to protect God's reputation by trying to look like we have it all together when we do not. If a climate of acceptance and openness to need is not established, God and the church community are hindered in their ability to be dynamic agents of healing and hope.

As God is worshiped in truth, accountability is established and this begins to help people walk upwardly; affirmation and healing are encouraged, and there is a natural expression of shared joy within the caring community. There will be opportunities provided for sharing that joy and an atmosphere of celebration and appreciation for the well-being that people are experiencing in the midst of life's struggles.

It seems to me that the functions of a Christian community as a true community, rather than a program-focused institution, would be greatly enhanced by actively drawing spiritually and emotionally mature women into the process of shaping and encouraging community. Without meaning to be sexist in any way, it does seem that, in general, women are more tuned to the relational dimension of life while men are more likely to be

task-oriented. Men are normally the decision-makers and for-
mulators of church functioning, as pastor, elders, and other
heads of functions. Their general tendency, however, is to look
at things pragmatically or politically rather than emotionally
and relationally. Perhaps the role of deaconess needs to be
broadened to include significant input and leadership for the
formation of community life within the local church. Perhaps
elders should be encouraged to include their wives in ministry to those under their care.

Suffering

The journey toward wholeness and *shalom* is, of course, not
a smooth one. Life is filled with distress that is not of our own
making. It is at the point of suffering that psychospiritual counseling and discipleship through the Christian community have
an opportunity to join hands in partnership.
    In an earlier work, I suggested that:

> At first glance, counseling and discipleship do not
> seem to be closely related. . . . When we look more
> closely, however, the differences between counseling
> and discipleship may not be as discrete as they
> appear. . . . The Bible teaches that suffering is an
> unavoidable part of the believer's life. Acknowledg-
> ing pain and constructively processing it are part of
> what it means to become a disciple of Jesus
> Christ. . . . Learning to live with the pain of life in
> constructive ways is part of psychospiritual growth
> and maturity. This growth may need to be helped
> by counseling, which is an essential component of
> discipleship in a context of suffering. . . . When we
> view counseling and discipleship as compatible
> components of growth and maturation we are able
> to accept people *as* they are and *where* they are from
> the beginning. As we see the relationship with
> counseling we are better able to incorporate the
> weaknesses and problems of real life into discipling.[36]

Helping people to process the pain of life without bitterness or fatalism and a victim's mentality is a significant aspect of counseling and discipleship that leads people to *shalom*.

Coming to grips with suffering in one's life involves accepting the fact that suffering is the fallout of the Fall. Pain-free life in a fallen world is impossible. And yet, it does seem that some people experience greater levels of suffering (that is not self-generated) than others. For example, Lydia did nothing to invite sexual abuse from her grandfather, stepfather, and brother while she was a young girl. Nor did she have any say in her mother's divorce and rejection of her. She did not ask to suffer with breast cancer when she was thirty-eight, nor for her son to be born physically handicapped. How does one counsel people like Lydia?

Perhaps the three most significant keys are helping the person to

1. accept that he or she is not being punished for being a bad person;
2. find meaning in the suffering;
3. forgive God and others.

First, counselees need help in evaluating the possible sources of their suffering. While it *may* be rooted in their patterns of living contrary to God's design, it is not necessarily due to God's punishment for their sin. Those who are highly passive and who struggle with issues of shame and low self-worth are those most likely to draw this conclusion.

The story of Jesus' interaction with the man who was born blind is instructive: "His disciples asked him, 'Rabbi, who sinned, this man or his parents, that he was born blind?' 'Neither this man nor his parents sinned,' said Jesus, 'but this happened so that the work of God might be displayed in his life'" (John 9:2–3). In other words, suffering is not necessarily God's punishment for sin. Paradoxically, bad things may even be allowed to demonstrate God's good purposes. Sometimes suffering is the simple result of the negative impact of the fallen world. Accidents do happen as a result of ignorance, unintended carelessness, and unfortunate timing. Disease and death happen to both saints and sinners.

Helping counselees find meaning in their suffering is also a vital intervention. Viktor Frankl formulated an entire system of logo therapy based on his observations and experience of the critical role that meaning played in the ability of people to survive the horrible suffering of World War II concentration camps.[37] The Apostle Paul reflected, "I consider that our present sufferings are not worth comparing with the glory that will be revealed in us" (Rom. 8:18). The ability to find meaning in the midst of suffering is essential if a person is going to be able to experience *shalom* in the midst of life's pain and victimization.

Finally, forgiving God and others requires reframing, or looking at the circumstances from a different point of view than that of a victim. Victimization breeds bitterness, and bitterness isolates a person from both God and others. Isolation, in turn, promotes Downward Path behaviors as the person is cut off from more balanced feedback and perspectives that come from intimate and accountable relationships. Reframing is the most difficult with people who have experienced a series of highly painful events in their lives. Helping the counselee to understand that God is not the giver of evil but the giver of choice is an important first step. One of the results of human choice was the Fall, which created total disorder throughout the creation. In addition, continuing sin choices are made by each of us. Sometimes we suffer because of other people's choices and sometimes because of our own. Sometimes suffering seems to be the outworking of the fallen order. Suffering is, indeed, the norm rather than the exception. Yet this is one of the hardest things for Americans to understand. We *expect* life to be relatively pain-free; we are encouraged to think that pills, potions, and antiperspirants can take all the pain away. The truth of the matter is that pain is inevitable and *can* bring out the best in us, that is, "the aroma of Christ" (2 Cor. 2:15) who suffered greatly and redemptively.

Psychospiritual counselors help counselees to see that Satan, the Grand Adversary of God and of those who bear God's image, attempts to overwhelm and paralyze people with bitterness over the unfairness and inequity of suffering. Much suffering *is* unfair and unwarranted, but allowing ourselves to become embittered by it only enslaves us. Accepting injustice and forgiving frees us to grow into Christ-likeness. "We also rejoice in our sufferings, because we know that suffering produces perseverance; perseverance, character; and character, hope" (Rom. 5:3–4).

OVERCOMING TOXIC FAITH

In their hard-hitting book, *Toxic Faith: Understanding and Overcoming Religious Addiction*, Stephen Arterburn and Jack Felton have thoroughly examined the nature of toxic or twisted faith.[38] Their aim is not to debunk or put down genuine faith but to try and distinguish between real faith and harmful beliefs that prevent the growth of healthy holiness. Among the toxic rules that establish and perpetuate unhealthy spirituality are those promoting mistrust, control, and perfectionism.

In my opinion, growth toward maturity and spiritual well-being is most handicapped by these issues. The first two I will group together as trust/control and love/power orientations.

People who have difficulty trusting will try to protect themselves by exaggerated attempts to control their world. They may withdraw or they may try to manage the behaviors of others in order to avoid pain. The origins of mistrust and control are undoubtedly developmental. If Erik Ericson is correct, experiences encountered during infancy of insensitive and inappropriate caretaking may lay the foundation for an orientation of basic mistrust toward life. Certainly, though, mistrust can develop at any point where there have been significant experiences of apparent betrayal. Socialization practices per se can also promote the need to control; certainly middle-class values of predictability and order encourage this.

The result is not only difficulty in relating to others, but difficulty in relating to God. If spiritual growth and well-being involve giving control of one's choices and life to the all-powerful God of the universe, mistrust and the need to control work against spiritual well-being. Even the divine mandate to manage the created order in Genesis 1:28 has been warped by the Fall; our tendency is to see the created order as our possession rather than our custodial responsibility.

The result is that we often slip into a power mode of living. In this mode we may justify questionable attitudes and actions because we are "just doing God's work." Or we may detach our power plays from the rest of our faith and see no inconsistency. Frequently, of course, the well-being of others is damaged by our own defensiveness, control attempts, and power plays. The Scripture clearly shows that the way of spiritual well-being is the way of sacrificial love. This is no more clearly seen than in the person of Jesus Christ:

> Your attitude should be the same as that of Christ Jesus: Who, being in very nature God, did not consider equality with God something to be grasped [power], but made himself nothing, taking the very nature of a servant, being made in human likeness. And being found in appearance as a man, he humbled himself and became obedient to death— even death on a cross! Therefore God exalted him to the highest place and gave him the name that is above every name.

> Philippians 2:5–9

A power and control orientation is unhealthy both for the person employing it as well as for those who are the object of its exercise. A trust and love orientation, one that is not naive but is rooted in faith in the God who is trustworthy and loves us so much that He will be with us to help through the difficulties of life and give us strength and courage, promotes spiritual well-being. The psychospiritual counselor works to bring about an appropriate balance of love and self-care, trust and self-control/ management that will encourage spiritual growth and health.

Perfectionism is another attempt at control that interferes with spiritual well-being. Perfectionism may be regarded as an obsessive personality type.[39] It is the attempt to live life in such a way that self-forgiveness will be unnecessary and feelings of condemnation will be avoided. Perfectionists attempt to exercise total control over themselves, other people, and events. The goal of complete control is to silence anxiety over possible pain that might be experienced in the absence of that total control. The problem is the exaggerated need for control based on the false belief that ultimate control is possible. By leaving no room for criticism, the perfectionist's sense of competence, acceptance, belonging, and security are apparently ensured. The problem, of course, is that no one is able to be totally perfect.

The amount of emotional energy invested in the attempt to be perfect, and the anxiety generated over possible failure, however, negatively affect the perfectionist's sense of well-being. Among the characteristics of perfectionism that depress one's sense of well-being are the

> fear of making errors, fear of making a wrong decision or choice, strong devotion to work, a need for order or firmly established routine, frugality, a need to know and follow the rules, emotional guardedness, a tendency to be stubborn or oppositional, a heightened sensitivity to being pressured or controlled by others, an inclination to worry, ruminate or doubt, a need to be above criticism—moral, professional, or personal, cautiousness, and a chronic inner pressure to use every minute productively.[40]

The perfectionist fears the possibility of being shamed, of being inadequate, and, consequently, of being rejected if there are any evident flaws. Perfectionists are their own worst critic and judge. Spiritual well-being does not thrive in the midst of this bound-up approach to life. Perfectionism makes life too serious for joy. The lack of self-acceptance and an inability to relax and just *be* imprison the person in a straitjacket of rigidity and unhappiness.

In many respects, perfectionism is based on a works-psychology that allows no room for grace because the acceptance of grace requires the admission of imperfection. Intervention must be focused on identifying false assumptions about what is necessary to be acceptable and accepted. Frequently, this requires a gentle look at parental standards and criticisms that have laid the foundation of the perfectionist personality. (Often perfectionists will be very protective of their parents, so the examination of parental patterns needs to be done sensitively.)

Counseling must also consider the issue of shame—the greatest fear of the perfectionist—and help the counselee to understand that imperfection is part of the disordered human condition rather than a unique flaw that requires condemnation and rejection.

CONFESSION

Perhaps the most liberating option available to fallen and imperfect human beings is the possibility of confession. The Bible gives the good news, "If we confess our sins, he [God] is faithful and just and will forgive us our sins and purify us from all unrighteousness" (1 John 1:9).

Because confession is made available to us, we neither have to pretend to be more than we are (perfect), nor do we have to suffer from feelings of shame and self-condemnation. Indeed, the Apostle John pointed out, "If we claim to be without sin, we deceive ourselves and the truth is not in us" (1 John 1:8).

Confession is essentially agreeing with God about our sin and our need to be forgiven. As we accept our fallen and flawed condition, we do not have to labor under the burden of self-generated psychomoral righteousness or the despair of failure. Confession is relinquishing both the myth of perfection and the crushing weight of guilt and judgment in exchange for the life-giving breath of God's love and mercy. It promotes an honest view of self that is accepted by a Greater Being and Judge than our selves or Satan. Consequently, we are able to experience *shalom* as confessional beings who are grateful for the gift of grace.

SPIRITUAL DISCIPLINE

Finally, spiritual well-being is promoted by commitment to a variety of spiritual disciplines.[41] In addition to the classic spiritual disciplines of prayer, Bible study, and fasting, it seems to me that biblically based and clearly Christian Twelve-Step groups can also be regarded as spiritual disciplines.[42] The Twelve-Step approach requires an ongoing commitment to accountability and honesty, constructive self-examination, recognition and acceptance of one's need for God's healing power, and appropriate restitution for offenses committed against others. This approach potentially provides for the contemporary Protestant evangelical a modern alternative to older Catholic practices of spiritual contemplative retreats.[43] The process of sharing one's journey and of having a sponsor who will mentor and walk with one as needed provides the strength to walk well.

Although spiritual disciplines are no more fun for most people than physical exercise (because of the effort required and Satan's attempts to divert), the after-effects are much the same: a greatly increased sense of spiritual well-being and general *shalom*.

NOTES

1. Craig W. Ellison, "Spiritual Well-Being: Conceptualization and Measurement," *Journal of Psychology and Theology* 11, no. 4 (1983): 331–32.

2. The Spiritual Well-Being Scale © 1982 by Craig W. Ellison and Raymond F. Paloutzian is available from Life Advance, Inc., 81 Front Street, Nyack, New York 10960. See Raymond F. Paloutzian and Craig W. Ellison, "Loneliness, Spiritual Well-Being and the Quality of Life," in *Loneliness: A Sourcebook of Current Theory, Research and Therapy*, ed. Letitia A. Peplau and Daniel Perlman (New York: Wiley-Interscience, 1982) for the initial published report of research and development of the Spiritual Well-Being Scale. See also Ellison, "Spiritual Well-Being," 330–40, which gives extensive theoretical, methodological, and early research information.

3. I especially want to note with appreciation the extensive research that has been developed and conducted by Dr. Rodger Bufford and his doctoral students at Western Conservative Baptist Seminary and, more recently, the graduate psychology program of George Fox College in Newberg, Oregon.

4. For the most recent published research update see Craig W. Ellison and Joel Smith, "Toward An Integrative Measure of Health and Well-Being," *Journal of Psychology and Theology* 19, no. 1 (Spring 1991): 35–48. The findings given in this chapter are primarily and extensively taken from that article.

5. D. Hawkins and R. Larson, "The Relationship between Measures of Health and Spiritual Well-Being" (manuscript, Western Conservative Baptist Seminary, 1984).

6. C. D. Campbell, "Coping with Hemodialysis: Cognitive Appraisals, Coping Behaviors, Spiritual Well-Being, Assertiveness, and Family Adaptability and Cohesion as Correlates of Adjustment," abstract in *Dissertation Abstracts International* 49 (1988): 538B.

7. J. Mickley, "Spiritual Well-Being, Religiousness and Hope: Some Relationships in a Sample of Women with Breast Cancer" (master's thesis, University of Maryland, School of Nursing, 1990).

8. V. B. Carson et al., "Hope and Spiritual Well-Being: Essentials for Living with AIDS," *Perspectives in Psychiatric Care* 26, no. 2 (1990).

9. V. B. Carson, "The Relationships of Spiritual Well-Being, Selected Demographic Variables, Health Indicators, and AIDS Related Activities to Hardiness in Persons Who were Serum Positive for the Human Immune Deficient Virus or Were Diagnosed with Acquired Immune Deficient Syndrome" (doctoral dissertation, University of Maryland, School of Nursing, 1990).

10. S. L. Granstrom, "A Comparative Study of Loneliness, Buberian Religiosity and Spiritual Well-Being in Cancer Patients" (paper presented at the annual conference of the National Hospice Organization, November 1987).

11. J. M. Kaczorowski, "Spiritual Well-Being and Anxiety in Adults Diagnosed with Cancer," *Hospice Journal* 5 (1989): 105–16.

12. C. M. Bonner, "Utilization of Spiritual Resources by Patients Experiencing a Recent Cancer Diagnosis" (master's thesis, University of Pittsburgh, 1988).

13. P. W. Kohlbry, "The Relationship between Spiritual Well-Being and Hope/Hopelessness in Chronically Ill Clients" (master's thesis, Marquette University, College of Nursing, 1986).

14. J. F. Miller, "Assessment of Loneliness and Spiritual Well-Being in Chronically Ill and Healthy Adults," *Journal of Professional Nursing* 2 (1985): 79–85.

15. N. J. G. Crumpler, "The Relationship between Spiritual Well-Being and Reported Self-Actualization among College Students" (master's thesis, East Carolina University, 1989).

16. S. Jang, T. Paddon, and W. Palmer, "Locus of Control in Relation to Spiritual Well-Being and Spiritual Maturity" (manuscript, Western Conservative Baptist Seminary, 1985).

17. Paloutzian and Ellison, "Loneliness."

18. V. B. Carson, K. L. Soeken, and P. M. Grimm, "Hope and Its Relationship to Spiritual Well-Being; Essentials for Living with AIDS," *Perspectives in Psychiatric Care* 26, no. 2 (1990); K. A. Herth, "An Abbreviated Instrument to Measure Hope" (manuscript, Northern Illinois University, 1989); Kohlbry, "Spiritual Well-Being and Hope/Hopelessness"; J. F. Miller and M. J. Powers, "Development of an Instrument to Measure Hope," *Nursing Research* 37 (1988): 6–10; W. C. Palmer, "Generalized Hope, Expectancies, Locus of Control, and Spiritual Well-Being in Relation to Quitting Smoking," abstract in *Dissertation Abstracts International* 48 (1988): 3691B.

19. R. J. Fehring, P. F. Brennan, and M. L. Keller, "Psychological and Spiritual Well-Being in College Students," *Research in Nursing and Health* 10 (1987).

20. D. Olson and K. L. Stewart, "Family Systems and Health Behaviors," in *New Directions in Health Psychology Assessment*, ed. H. Schroeder (Bristol, Penn.: Hemisphere, 1991), 27–64.

21. J. L. Frantz, "MMPI and DSM-III Diagnosis Related to Selected Measures of Religious and Demographic Variables in Adult Outpatients," abstract in *Dissertation Abstracts International* 48 (1988): 3678B.

22. R. K. Bufford and T. G. Parker, "Religion and Well-Being: Concurrent Validation of the Spiritual Well-Being Scale" (paper presented at the annual meeting of the American Psychological Association, Los Angeles, California, 1985); D. B. Hawkins, "Interpersonal Behavior Traits, Spiritual Well-Being, and Their Relationships to Blood Pressure," abstract in *Dissertation Abstracts International* 48 (1988): 3680B.

23. C. D. Campbell, W. H. Mullins, and J. Colwell, "Spiritual Well-Being Assertiveness: A Correlation Study" (manuscript, Western Conservative Baptist Seminary, 1984).

24. Paloutzian and Ellison, "Loneliness"; M. L. Durham, "Denominational Differences in Attribution to Supernatural Causation" (manuscript, Western Conservative Baptist Seminary, 1984).

25. Frantz, "MMPI and DSM-III Diagnosis."

26. Granstrom, "A Comparative Study."

27. B. Ewing, T. Parker, and J. Quinn, "Correlates of the Spiritual Leadership Qualities Inventory, the Religious Orientation Scale, and the Spiritual Well-Being Scale" (manuscript, Western Conservative Baptist Seminary, 1983).

28. Craig W. Ellison et al., "Personality, Religious Orientation, and Spiritual Well-Being" (manuscript, Alliance Theological Seminary, 1984).

29. R. K. Bufford, "Empirical Correlations of Spiritual Well-Being and Spiritual Maturity Scales" (paper presented at the annual meeting of the Christian Association for Psychological Studies, Dallas, Texas, 1984); Granstrom, "A Comparative Study."

30. M. L. Durham, "Denominational Differences in Supernatural Locus of Control and Spiritual Well-Being," abstract in *Dissertation Abstracts International* 48 (1988): 3714B.

31. Bufford, "Empirical Correlations"; Granstrom, "A Comparative Study."

32. Bufford, "Empirical Correlations."

33. I am grateful for the insightful analysis of Lehman Strauss regarding Jehovah-Shalom (the Lord My Peace) provided in his book, *The Godhead: Devotional Studies on the Three Persons of the Trinity* (Neptune, N. J.: Loizeaux Brothers, 1990). My comments in this section are undergirded by Dr. Strauss's careful study.

34. Strauss, *The Godhead*, 181.

35. See Evelyn E. Whitehead and James D. Whitehead, *Seasons of Strength: New Visions of Adult Maturing* (New York: Doubleday, 1986) for a fascinating discussion of vocation as a lifelong conversation with God.

36. See Craig W. Ellison and Edward S. Maynard, *Healing for the City: Counseling in the Urban Setting* (Grand Rapids: Zondervan, 1992), 48–50; see also Craig W. Ellison, "Counseling and Discipleship for the City" in *Discipling the City*, 2d ed., ed. Roger S. Greenway (Grand Rapids: Baker, 1992), 99–110.

37. Viktor E. Frankl, *Man's Search for Meaning* (New York: Washington Square, 1970). Other helpful books on helping counselees to find meaning are Joseph Fabry, *Guideposts to Meaning* (Oakland, Calif.: New Harbinger, 1988); and Paul R. Welter, *Counseling and the Search for Meaning* (Dallas: Word, 1987).

38. Stephen Arterburn and Jack Felton, *Toxic Faith: Understanding and Overcoming Religious Addiction* (Nashville: Thomas Nelson, 1991).

39. See Allan E. Mallinger and Jeannette DeWyze, *Too Perfect: When Being in Control Gets Out of Control* (New York: Clarkson Potter, 1992) for a clear, cogent, and detailed analysis, along with practical guidelines for counseling the perfectionist. My comments are partially based upon their observations.

40. Ibid., 3.

41. See Richard Foster, *The Celebration of Discipline* (San Francisco: Harper and Row, 1978) for a detailed and excellent treatment of the spiritual disciplines.

42. If we view the Twelve-Step approach as part of spiritual discipline, churches should become increasingly active in establishing and encouraging involvement in such groups. Many helpful resources are available today through such groups as the National Association of Christians in Recovery, P. O. Box 11095, Whittier, California 90603-3718. (The National Association of Christians in Recovery will also help you get in touch with Christian self-help groups).

43. Bernard J. Tyrrell, S. J. *Christotherapy II* (Ramsey, N. J.: Paulist Press, 1982).

Appendix One

Psychospiritual Needs Inventory

Please indicate how characteristic each statement is of you by circling the appropriate response by the statement.

SA = Strongly Agree	D = Slightly Disagree
MA = Moderately Agree	MD = Moderately Disagree
A = Slightly Agree	SD = Strongly Disagree
N = Neither agree nor disagree	

1. I feel good about myself. SA MA A N D MD SD

2. My relationships are
   usually long-term. SA MA A N D MD SD

3. I am good at what I do. SA MA A N D MD SD

4. Life is basically fair. SA MA A N D MD SD

5. I have a good sense of
   who I am. SA MA A N D MD SD

6. I feel calm and assured
   about life.   SA MA A N D MD SD

7. I feel like I am a worthwhile
   person.   SA MA A N · D MD SD

8. There is more to life than
   living for the moment.   SA MA A N D MD SD

9. I often feel guilty.   SA MA A N D MD SD

10. I often feel lonely.   SA MA A N D MD SD

11. I am not very talented.   SA MA A N D MD SD

12. I have been harmed by others
    who took advantage
    of me.   SA MA A N D MD SD

13. My life seems aimless.   SA MA A N D MD SD

14. I often worry that something
    bad will happen to me.   SA MA A N D MD SD

15. My life isn't worth
    very much.   SA MA A N D MD SD

16. I am getting nothing out
    of life.   SA MA A N D MD SD

17. People usually like me.   SA MA A N D MD SD

18. The relationships I am
    involved in are rewarding. SA MA A N D MD SD

19. I like challenges.   SA MA A N D MD SD

20. People can usually be trusted. SA MA A N D MD SD

21. I have a definite set of values
    that I am committed to.   SA MA A N D MD SD

22. I usually feel safe.   SA MA A N D MD SD

23. Others seek me out for my
    thoughts on things.   SA MA A N D MD SD

24. I have a satisfying
    relationship with God.   SA MA A N D MD SD

25. Usually I wish I were
    someone else.   SA MA A N D MD SD

26. I rarely feel satisfied in my
    relationships.   SA MA A N D MD SD

27. I have good intentions but
    I have trouble making
    things happen.   SA MA A N D MD SD

28. People are often exploitative
    and use others for their
    own gain.   SA MA A N D MD SD

29. I am often confused about
    what I really think or feel. SA MA A N D MD SD

30. Often I feel anxious.   SA MA A N D MD SD

31. I often feel insignificant
    or worthless.   SA MA A N D MD SD

32. God seems very irrelevant
    to my life.   SA MA A N D MD SD

33. I am basically pleased with
    who I am.   SA MA A N D MD SD

34. My relationships are
    mutually satisfying.   SA MA A N D MD SD

35. I think I could succeed at
    anything I set my mind to. SA MA A N D MD SD

36. People are normally kind
    or compassionate.   SA MA A N D MD SD

37. I have a clear idea about
    where I am headed in life. SA MA A N D MD SD

38. My close relationships
    basically give me a
    feeling of peace.   SA MA A N D MD SD

39. I feel like my life is making
    a difference.   SA MA A N D MD SD

40. My life has a sense of ulti-
    mate meaning or purpose. SA MA A N D MD SD

41. I feel like my family has
    always rejected me.   SA MA A N D MD SD

42. I feel distant from
other people. SA MA A N D MD SD

43. I am reluctant to try new
things for fear I will fail. SA MA A N D MD SD

44. People are frequently
manipulative or scheming. SA MA A N D MD SD

45. I do things for reasons I
don't understand. SA MA A N D MD SD

46. I seldom feel really safe
or secure. SA MA A N D MD SD

47. My thoughts and feelings
don't seem to count
for much. SA MA A N D MD SD

48. I live life focusing on the
here and now. SA MA A N D MD SD

49. What others think of me
doesn't significantly affect
how I feel about myself. SA MA A N D MD SD

50. I feel like other people enjoy
being my friends. SA MA A N D MD SD

51. I feel like I am able to effectively manage my life. SA MA A N D MD SD

52. Most people act reasonably
toward others. SA MA A N D MD SD

53. I have a satisfying personal
philosophy of life. SA MA A N D MD SD

54. My life is filled with a
sense of well-being. SA MA A N D MD SD

55. I feel like I am valued
by others. SA MA A N D MD SD

56. I feel in tune with life. SA MA A N D MD SD

57. I feel like there is something
wrong with who I am. SA MA A N D MD SD

58. I would rather be by myself
    than with other people.   SA MA A N D MD SD

59. Other people are usually
    more competent than
    I am.   SA MA A N D MD SD

60. My decisions don't really
    seem to have much effect
    on what actually happens
    to me.   SA MA A N D MD SD

61. I feel like I don't know
    who I am.   SA MA A N D MD SD

62. I feel like my life is very
    fragile.   SA MA A N D MD SD

63. I could disappear and no
    one would really miss me. SA MA A N D MD SD

64. My life doesn't have a sense
    of ultimate purpose.   SA MA A N D MD SD

65. I feel like I am accepted
    for who I am.   SA MA A N D MD SD

66. Having friends is very
    important to me.   SA MA A N D MD SD

67. My decisions are generally
    good ones.   SA MA A N D MD SD

68. Justice usually prevails in
    human affairs.   SA MA A N D MD SD

69. I am satisfied with who I am. SA MA A N D MD SD

70. I seldom worry about what
    is happening in my life.   SA MA A N D MD SD

71. I feel like I matter.   SA MA A N D MD SD

72. My relationship with God
    gives me a sense of
    purpose in life.   SA MA A N D MD SD

73. I feel like I'm an unwanted
    bother.   SA MA A N D MD SD

74. I fantasize quite often.   SA MA A N D MD SD

75. It seems like I do poorly at
    everything I try.   SA MA A N D MD SD

76. It seems to me that justice
    is more of a myth than a
    reality.   SA MA A N D MD SD

77. I feel like I try to be what
    others want me to be and
    end up without a sense of
    my self.   SA MA A N D MD SD

78. I do a lot of worrying about
    what might happen in
    the future.   SA MA A N D MD SD

79. I basically feel like no one
    needs me.   SA MA A N D MD SD

80. Life seems to have no real
    meaning other than
    staying alive.   SA MA A N D MD SD

81. My life is in constant turmoil. SA MA A N D MD SD

82. Most of my decisions are
    based on my immediate
    desires, rather than on
    long-range values.   SA MA A N D MD SD

Appendix Two

Spiritual Well-Being Scale

For each of the following statements, *circle* the choice that best indicates the extent of your agreement or disagreement as it describes your personal experience:

SA = Strongly Agree   D = Slightly Disagree
MA = Moderately Agree   MD = Moderately Disagree
A = Slightly Agree   SD = Strongly Disagree

1. I don't find much satisfaction in private prayer with God.

    SA MA A D MD SD

2. I don't know who I am, where I came from, or where I'm going.

    SA MA A D MD SD

3. I believe that God loves me and cares about me.

    SA MA A D MD SD

4. I feel that life is a positive experience.

    SA MA A D MD SD

5. I believe that God is impersonal and not interested in my daily situation.

    SA MA A D MD SD

6. I feel unsettled about my future.

    SA MA A D MD SD

7. I have a personally meaningful relationship with God.

    SA MA A D MD SD

8. I feel very fulfilled and
    satisfied with life.   SA MA A D MD SD

9. I don't get much personal
    strength and support from
    my God.   SA MA A D MD SD

10. I feel a sense of well-being
    about the direction my
    life is headed.   SA MA A D MD SD

11. I believe that God is concerned
    about my problems.   SA MA A D MD SD

12. I don't enjoy much about life. SA MA A D MD SD

13. I don't have a personally
    satisfying relationship
    with God.   SA MA A D MD SD

14. I feel good about my future.   SA MA A D MD SD

15. My relationship with God
    helps me not to feel lonely.   SA MA A D MD SD

16. I feel that life is full of conflict
    and unhappiness.   SA MA A D MD SD

17. I feel most fulfilled when
    I'm in close communion
    with God.   SA MA A D MD SD

18. Life doesn't have much
    meaning.   SA MA A D MD SD

19. My relation with God
    contributes to my sense
    of well-being.   SA MA A D MD SD

20. I believe there is some real
    purpose for my life.   SA MA A D MD SD

Bibliography

Abplanalp, Judith M. "Psychosocial Theories." In *PMS: Premenstrual Syndrome*, ed. William R. Keye. Philadelphia: Saunders, 1988.

Adams, D. *Understanding and Managing Stress*. San Diego: University Associates, Inc., 1980.

Adler, Tina. "Social Factors Link Hostility, Illness." *APA Monitor* (January 1991).

American Psychiatric Association. *Diagnostic and Statistical Manual of Mental Disorders*. 3d. rev. ed. Washington, D. C.: American Psychiatric Association, 1987.

————. *Quick Reference to the Diagnostic Criteria from DSM III-R*. Washington, D. C.: American Psychiatric Association, 1987.

Anderson, Marcia, Leigh Flynn, Beth Mattsson-Boze, and Deborah Vassallo. "Stress in the Lives of Women." Manuscript, Alliance Theological Seminary, December 1990.

Anderson, Ray S. *On Being Human: Essays in Theological Anthropology*. Grand Rapids: Eerdmans, 1982.

————. *Christians Who Counsel: The Vocation of Wholistic Therapy*. Grand Rapids: Zondervan, 1990.

Arterburn, Stephen, and Jack Felton. *Toxic Faith: Understanding and Overcoming Religious Addiction*. Nashville: Thomas Nelson, 1991.

Barnett, R. C., L. Biener, and G. K. Baruch. *Gender and Stress*. New York: The Free Press, 1987.

Belle, Deborah. "Gender Differences in Social Moderators of Stress." In *Gender and Stress*, ed. R. C. Barnett, L. Bienner, and G. K. Baruch. New York: The Free Press, 1987.

Birkedahl, Nonie. *The Habit Control Workbook*. Oakland, Calif.: New Harbinger Publications, 1990.

Bonner, C. M., "Utilization of Spiritual Resources by Patients Experiencing a Recent Cancer Diagnosis." Master's thesis, University of Pittsburgh, 1988.

Brady, Kathleen, Elizabeth Taylor, and James Willwerth. "Struggling for Sanity." *Time* 8 October 1990.

Buckley, Francis J., S. J., and Donald B. Sharp, S. J. *Deepening Christian Life*. San Francisco: Harper and Row, 1987.

Bufford, R. K. "Empirical Correlations of Spiritual Well-Being and Spiritual Maturity Scales." Paper presented at the annual meeting of the Christian Association for Psychological Studies, Dallas, Texas, 1984.

Bufford, R. K., and T. G. Parker. "Religion and Well-Being: Concurrent Validation of the Spiritual Well-Being Scale." Paper presented at the annual meeting of the American Psychological Association, Los Angeles, California, 1985.

Bugental, James F. T. *The Search for Authenticity*. New York: Holt, Rinehart and Winston, 1965.

————. *The Search for Authenticity*. Rev. ed. New York: Irvington, 1981.

Bullard, D. M., H. H. Glaser, M. C. Heagarty, and E. C. Pivcheck. "Failure to Thrive in the Neglected Child." *American Journal of Orthopsychiatry* 37 (1967).

Campbell, C. D. "Coping with Hemodialysis: Cognitive Appraisals, Coping Behaviors, Spiritual Well-Being, Assertiveness, and Family Adaptability and Cohesion as Correlates of Adjustment." Abstract in *Dissertation Abstracts International* 49 (1988): 538B.

Campbell, C. D., W. H. Mullins, and J. Colwell."Spiritual Well-Being Assertiveness: A Correlation Study." Manuscript, Western Conservative Baptist Seminary, 1984.

Carson, V. B. "The Relationships of Spiritual Well-Being, Selected Demographic Variables, Health Indicators, and AIDS Related Activities to Hardiness in Persons Who Were Serum Positive for the Human Immune Deficient Virus or Were Diagnosed with Acquired Immune Deficient Syndrome." Doctoral diss. University of Maryland, School of Nursing, 1990.

Carson, V. B., K. L. Soeken, and P. M. Grimm. "Hope and Its Relationship to Spiritual Well-Being." *Journal of Psychology and Theology* 16 (1988).

Carson, V. B., K. L. Soeken, J. Shanty, and L. Toms. "Hope and Spiritual Well-Being: Essentials for Living with AIDS." *Perspectives in Psychiatric Care* 26, no. 2 (1990).

Chess, Stella. "Pathogenesis of the Adjustment Disorders: Vulnerabilities due to Temperamental Factors." In *Stressors and the Adjustment Disorders*, ed. Joseph D. Noshpitz and R. Dean Coddington. New York: Wiley, 1990.

Chess, S., A. Thomas, and H. G. Birch. *Your Child Is A Person*. New York: Viking, 1965.

Coleman, James C., James N. Butcher, and Robert C. Carson. *Abnormal Psychology and Modern Life*. Glenview, Ill.: Scott Foresman, 1980.

Conway, Jim. *Adult Children of Legal or Emotional Divorce: Healing Your Long-Term Hurt*. Downers Grove: InterVarsity, 1990.

Cotton, Dorothy H. G. *Stress Management: An Integrated Approach to Therapy*. New York: Brunner-Mazel, 1990.

Crumpler, N. J. G. "The Relationship between Spiritual Well-Being and Reported Self-Actualization among College Students." Master's thesis, East Carolina University, 1989.

Danish, Steven J., Anthony R. D'Augelli, and Allen L. Hauer. *Helping Skills: A Basic Training Program, Trainee's Workbook*. 2d ed. New York: Human Sciences Press, 1980.

DeAngelis, Tori. "Living with Violence: Children Suffer, Cope." *APA Monitor* (January 1991).

Dufton, B. D., and D. Perlman. "The Association between Religiosity and the Purpose in Life Test: Does It Reflect

Purpose or Satisfaction?" *Journal of Psychology and Theology* 14 (1986).

Durham, M. L., "Denominational Differences in Attribution to Supernatural Causation." Manuscript, Western Conservative Baptist Seminary, 1984.

————. "Denominational Differences in Supernatural Locus of Control and Spiritual Well-Being." In *Dissertation Abstracts International* 48 (1988): 3714B.

Eaton, Rebecca, and Deborah Moon. "Uncovering the Truth and Myth about PMS." Project, Alliance Theological Seminary, December 1990.

Egan, Gerald. *The Skilled Helper*, 4th ed. Pacific Grove, Calif.: Brooks/Cole, 1990.

Elliott, G. R., and C. Eisdorfer. *Stress and Human Health.* New York: Springer, 1982.

Ellison, Craig W.. *Saying Goodbye to Loneliness and Finding Intimacy*. San Francisco: Harper and Row, 1983.

————. "Spiritual Well-Being: Conceptualization and Measurement." *Journal of Psychology and Theology* 11 no. 4 (1983): 330–40.

————. "Self-Esteem." In *Baker Encyclopedia of Psychology*, ed. David G. Benner. Grand Rapids: Baker, 1985.

————. "The War of the Ages." Manuscript, Alliance Theological Seminary, 1988.

————. "Counseling and Discipleship for the City." In *Discipling the City*, ed. Roger S. Greenway. 2d ed. Grand Rapids: Baker, 1993.

————. *Psychospiritual Needs Inventory; Spiritual Well-Being Scale; Spiritual Maturity Index*. Alliance Theological Seminary, 350 North Highland Avenue, Nyack, New York 10960 or New Hope Counseling Center, 68–60 Austin Street, Suite 301, Forest Hills, New York 11355.

————. ed. *Your Better Self: Christianity, Psychology and Self-Esteem*. San Francisco: Harper and Row, 1983.

Ellison, Craig W., and Edward S. Maynard. *Healing for the City: Counseling for the Urban Context*. Grand Rapids: Zondervan, 1992.

Ellison, Craig W., and Joel Smith. "Toward an Integrative Measure of Health and Well-Being." *Journal of Psychology and Theology* 19, no. 1, (Spring 1991): 35–48.

Ellison, Craig W., Imran Rashid, Patricia Patla, Reuel Calica, and Diana Haberman. "Personality, Religious Oreintation, and Spiritual Well-Being." Manuscript, Alliance Theological Seminary, 1984.

Ewing, B., T. Parker, and J. Quinn. "Correlates of the Spiritual Leadership Qualities Inventory, the Religious Orientation Scale, and the Spiritual Well-Being Scale." Manuscript, Western Conservative Baptist Seminary, 1983.

Fabry, Joseph. *Guideposts to Meaning*. Oakland, Calif.: New Harbinger, 1988.

Fehring, R. J., P. F. Brennan, and M. L. Keller. "Psychological and Spiritual Well-Being in College Students." *Research in Nursing and Health* 10 (1987).

Fossum, Merle A., and Marilyn J. Mason. *Facing Shame: Families in Recovery*. New York: Norton, 1986.

Foster, Richard. *The Celebration of Discipline*. San Francisco: Harper and Row, 1978.

Frank, Jan. *A Door of Hope: Recognizing and Resolving the Pains of Your Past*. San Bernardino, Calif.: Here's Life, 1987.

Frankl, Viktor E. *Man's Search for Meaning*. New York: Washington Square Press, 1970.

Frantz, J. L., "MMPI and DSM-III Diagnosis Related to Selected Measures of Religous and Demographic Variables in Adult Outpatients." Abstract in *Dissertation Abstracts International* 48 (1988): 3678B.

Freiberg, Peter. "Study: Disorders Found in 20 Percent of Children." *APA Monitor* (February 1991).

————. "Self-Esteem Gender Gap Widens in Adolescence." *APA Monitor* (April 1991).

Friesen, James G. *Uncovering the Mystery of MPD*. San Bernardino, Calif.: Here's Life, 1991.

Fromm, Erich. "Value, Psychology and Human Existence." In *New Knowledge in Human Values*, ed. A. H. Maslow. New York: Harper and Row, 1959.

Gardner, Richard A. "Childhood Stress Due to Parental Divorce." In *Stressors and the Adjustment Disorders*, ed. Joseph D. Noshpitz and R. Dean Coddington. New York: Wiley, 1990.

Gartner, J., D. B. Larson, and G. D. Allen. "Religious Commitment and Mental Health: A Review of the Empirical

Literature." *Journal of Psychology and Theology* 19 (1991).

Gibbs, Nancy. "How America Has Run Out of Time." *Time* 24 April 1989.

Granstrom, S. L. "A Comparative Study of Loneliness, Buberian Religiosity and Spiritual Well-Being in Cancer Patients." Paper presented at the annual conference of the National Hospice Organization, November 1987.

Hadaway, C. K. "Life Satisfaction and Religion: A Re-Analysis." *Social Forces* 57 (1978).

Harper, James M., and Margaret H. Hoopes. *Uncovering Shame: An Approach to Integrating Individuals and Their Family Systems.* New York: Norton, 1990.

Harris, R. L., G. L. Archer, and B. K. Waltke, eds. *Theological Wordbook of the Old Testament.* Vol. 2. Chicago: Moody, 1980.

Hawkins, D. B., "Interpersonal Behavior Traits, Spiritual Well-Being, and Their Relationships to Blood Pressure." Abstract in *Dissertation Abstracts International* 48 (1988): 3680B.

Hawkins, D., and R. Larson. "The Relationship between Measures of Health and Spiritual Well-Being." Manuscript, Western Conservative Baptist Seminary, 1984.

Herth, K. A. "An Abbreviated Instrument to Measure Hope." Manuscript, Northern Illinois University, 1989.

Hjelle, L. A., and D. J. Ziegler. *Personality Theories: Basic Assumptions, Research, and Applications.* New York: McGraw Hill, 1981.

Hoff, Lee Ann. *People in Crisis: Understanding and Helping.* Redwood City, Calif.: Addison-Wesley, 1989.

Holmes, Thomas H., and R. H. Rahe. "The Social Readjustment Rating Scale." *Journal of Psychosomatic Research* 11 (1967).

Howard, J. K. "The Concept of the Soul in Psychology and Religion." *Journal of the American Scientific Affiliation* 24 (1972).

Jang, S., T. Paddon, and W. Palmer. "Locus of Control in Relation to Spiritual Well-Being and Spiritual Maturity." Manuscript, Western Conservative Baptist Seminary, 1985.

Johnson, Kendall. *Trauma in the Lives of Children: Crisis and Stress Management Techniques for Counselors and Other Professionals.* Claremont, Calif.: Hunter House, 1989.

Jones, James M. "Stress at Work Takes Costly Toll." *APA Monitor* 21, no. 9 (September 1990).

Justice, Jr., William G. *Guilt and Forgiveness: How God Can Help You Feel Good about Yourself.* Grand Rapids: Baker, 1980.

Kaczorowski, J. M., "Spiritual Well-Being and Anxiety in Adults Diagnosed with Cancer." *Hospice Journal* 5 (1989): 105–16.

Keller, John E. *Let Go, Let God: Surrendering Self-Centered Delusions in the Costly Journey of Faith.* Minneapolis: Augsburg, 1985.

Kittel, G. ed. *Theological Dictionary of the New Testament,* trans. and ed. Geoffrey W. Bromiley. Vol. 2. Grand Rapids: Eerdmans, 1964.

Kohlbry, P. W. "The Relationship between Spiritual Well-Being and Hope/Hopelessnes in Chronically Ill Clients." Master's thesis, Marquette University, College of Nursing, 1986.

Kutash, Irwin L., Louis B. Schlesinger, and Associates, *Handbook on Stress and Anxiety.* San Francisco: Jossey-Bass, 1980.

Lawlor, Julia. "Stress, Computer Squeal Linked." *USA Today,* 21 August 1990, reporting on research by Douglas Covert and Caroline Dow, Dept. of Communications, University of Evansville, Ind.

Lazarus, R. S., and S. Folkman. *Stress, Appraisal and Coping.* New York: Springer, 1984.

Maddi, S. R. *Personality Theories: A Comparative Analysis.* Homewood, Ill.: Dorsey, 1976.

Mallinger, Allan E., and Jeannette DeWyze. *Too Perfect: When Being in Control Gets Out of Control.* New York: Clarkson Potter, 1992.

Marlin, Emily. *Genograms: The New Tool for Exploring the Personality, Career and Love Patterns You Inherit.* New York: Contemporary Books, 1989.

Martin, Grant L. *Counseling for Family Violence and Abuse.* Dallas: Word, 1987.

Maslow, Abraham. *Motivation and Personality.* 2d ed. New York: Harper and Row, 1970.

Matteson, Michael T., and John M. Ivancevich. *Controlling Work Stress: Effective Human Resource and Management Strategies.* San Francisco: Jossey-Bass, 1987.

McGoldrick, Monica, and Randy Gerson. *Genograms in Family Assessment*. New York: Norton, 1985.

McGuire, Kent. "Adult Children of Divorce: Curative Factors of Support Group Therapy." Doctoral research paper presented to the faculty of the Rosemead Graduate School of Psychology, Biola University, La Mirada, Calif., May 1987.

Messina, James J. *Tools for Communications; Tools for Relationships*. Tampa, Fl.: Advanced Development Systems, 1989.

Mickley, J. "Spiritual Well-Being, Religiousness and Hope: Some Relationships in a Sample of Women with Breast Cancer." Master's thesis, University of Maryland, School of Nursing, 1990.

Miller, J. F. "Assessment of Loneliness and Spiritual Well-Being in Chronically Ill and Healthy Adults." *Journal of Professional Nursing* 2 (1985): 79–85.

Miller, J. F., and M. J. Powers. "Development of an Instrument to Measure Hope." *Nursing Research* 37 (1988): 6–10.

Moberg, David O. *Spiritual Well-Being: Sociological Perspectives*. Washington, D. C.: University Press of America, 1979.

Morse, Donald R., and M. Lawrence Furst. *Women Under Stress*. New York: Van Nostrand Reinhold, 1982.

Narramore, S. Bruce. *No Condemnation*. Grand Rapids: Zondervan, 1985.

Noshpitz, Joseph D., and R. Dean Coddington, eds. *Stress and the Adjustment Disorders*. New York: Wiley, 1990.

Olson, D., and K. L. Stewart. "Family Systems and Health Behaviors." In *New Directions in Health Psychology Assessment*, ed. Harold Schroeder. Bristol, Penn.: Hemisphere Publishing, 1991.

"Outrage." National Resources Defense Council Newsletter (February 1991).

Palmer, W. C., "Generalized Hope, Expectancies, Locus of Control, and Spiritual Well-Being in Relation to Quitting Smoking." Abstract in *Dissertation Abstracts International* 48 (1988): 3691B.

Paloutzian, Raymond F., and Craig W. Ellison, "Loneliness, Spiritual Well-Being and the Quality of Life." In *Loneliness: A Sourcebook of Current Theory, Research and Therapy*, ed. Letitia A. Peplau and Daniel Perlman. New York: Wiley-Interscience, 1982.

Peterson, L. R., and A. Roy. "Religiosity, Anxiety, and Meaning and Purpose: Religion's Consequences for Psychological Well-Being." *Review of Religious Research* 27 (1985).

Potter-Efron, Ronald, and Patricia Potter-Efron. *Letting Go of Shame: Understanding How Shame Affects Your Life.* San Francisco: Harper and Row, 1989.

Preston, C. A., and L. L. Viney. "Construing God: An Exploration of the Relationship between Reported Interaction with God and Concurrent Emotional Experience." *Journal of Psychology and Theology* 14 (1986).

Prugh, D. G., and C. K. Taguiri. "Emotional Aspects of the Respirator Care of Patients with Poliomyelitis." *Psychosomatic Medicine* 42 (1954).

Prugh, Dane G., and Troy L. Thompson II. "Illness as a Source of Stress: Acute Illness, Chronic Illness, and Surgical Procedures." In *Stressors and the Adjustment Disorders,* ed. Joseph D. Noshpitz and R. Dean Coddington. New York: Wiley, 1990.

Reid, William H., and Michael G. Wise. *DSM-III-R Training Guide.* New York: Brunner-Mazel, 1989.

Roskies, Ethel. *Stress Management for the Healthy Type A: Theory and Practice.* New York: Guilford, 1987.

Rotton, J. "The Psychological Effects of Air Pollution." Manuscript, Florida International University, 1978.

————. "Affective Cognitive Consequences of Malodorous Pollution." *Basic and Applied Social Psychology* 4 (1983).

Rotton, J., J. Frey, R. Barry, M. Milligan, and M. Fitzpatrick. "The Air Pollution Experience and Physical Aggression." *Journal of Applied Social Psychology* 9 (1979).

Rotton J., and J. Frey. "Air Pollution, Weather and Psychiatric Emergencies: A Constructive Replication." Paper presented at the American Psychological Association: Washington, D. C., 1982.

Sanford, J. A. *Healing and Wholeness.* New York: Paulist Press, 1977.

Schreck, G. Peter. "Personhood and Relational Life Tasks: A Model for Integrating Psychology and Theology." In *Family Therapy: Christian Perspectives,* ed. Hendrika Vande Kempe. Grand Rapids: Baker, 1991.

Seamands, David. *Healing Grace.* Wheaton: Victor, 1988.

Sehnert, Keith W. *Stress/Unstress: How You Can Control Stress at Home and on the Job.* Minneapolis: Augsburg, 1981.

Selye, Hans. *The Stress of Life.* New York: McGraw-Hill, 1956.

————. *Stress without Distress.* New York: Lippincott and Crowell, 1974.

————. "The Stress Concept Today." In *Handbook on Stress and Anxiety,* ed. Irwin L. Kutash, Louis B. Schlesinger, and Associates. San Francisco: Jossey-Bass, 1980.

Skodol, Andrew E., Bruce P. Dohrenwend, Bruce G. Link, and Patrick E. Shrout. "The Nature of Stress: Problems of Measurement." In *Stressors and the Adjustment Disorders,* ed. Joseph D. Noshpitz and R. Dean Coddington. New York: Wiley, 1990.

Spitzer, Robert L., Miriam Gibbon, Andrew E. Skodol, Janet B. W. Williams, and Michael B. First. *DSM-III-R Case Book.* Washington, D. C.: American Psychiatric Press, 1989.

Stacey, D. W. *The Pauline View of Man.* London: MacMillan, 1956.

Strahilevitz, N., A. Strahilevitz, and J. E. Miller. "Air Pollution and the Admission Rate of Psychiatric Patients." *American Journal of Psychiatry* 136 (1978).

Strauss, Lehman. *The Godhead: Devotional Studies on the Three Persons of the Trinity.* Neptune, N. J.: Loizeaux Brothers, 1990.

Swihart, Judson. *How Do You Say I Love You?* Downers Grove: InterVarsity, 1977.

Thomas, A., and Chess, S. "Behavioral Individuality in Childhood." In *Development and Evolution of Behavior,* ed. L. R. Aronson, E. Tobach, D. S. Lehrman, and J. S. Rosenblatt. San Francisco: Freeman, 1970.

————. *Temperament and Development.* New York: Brunner-Mazel, 1977.

————. *The Dynamics of Psychological Development.* New York: Brunner-Mazel, 1980.

Thomas, A., S. Chess, and H. G. Birch. *Temperament and Behavior Disorders in Children.* New York: New York University Press, 1968.

————. "The Origin of Personality." *Scientific American* 223 (1970).

Thompson, Jeffrey. Unpublished communication, July 1990.

Thurman, Chris. *The Lies We Believe*. Nashville: Thomas Nelson, 1989.

Tillich, Paul. *The Courage to Be*. New Haven: Yale University Press, 1952.

Tyrrell, Bernard J. *Christotherapy II: A New Horizon for Counselors, Spiritual Directors and Seekers of Healing and Growth in Christ*. Ramsey, N. J.: Paulist Press, 1982.

Wallerstein, Judith S., and Sandra Blakeslee. *Second Chances: Men, Women and Children a Decade after Divorce*. New York: Ticknor and Fields, 1989.

Watson, P. J., R. J. Morris, and R. W. Jood, Jr. "Sin and Self-Functioning, Part 2: Grace, Guilt, and Psychological Adjustment." *Journal of Psychology and Theology* 16 (1988).

————. "Intrinsicness, Self-Actualization, and the Ideological Surround." *Journal of Psychology and Theology* 19 (1990).

Welter, Paul R. *Counseling and the Search for Meaning*. Dallas: Word, 1987.

Whitehead, Evelyn E., and James D. Whitehead. *Seasons of Strength: New Visions of Adult Maturing*. New York: Doubleday, 1986.

Whitlock, Glenn E. "The Structure of Personality in Hebrew Psychology." In *Wholeness and Holiness*, ed. H. Newton Malony. Grand Rapids: Baker, 1983, 41–45.

Wilson, Sandra D. *Released from Shame: Recovery for Adult Children of Dysfunctional Families*. Downers Grove: InterVarsity, 1990.

Wuertzer, Patricia, and Lucinda May. *Relax, Recover: Stress Management for Recovering People*. Minneapolis: Hazelden, 1988.

Subject Index

About the Author

Dr. Craig W. Ellison is Professor of Counseling and Urban Studies at The Alliance Theological Seminary in Nyack, New York. He is also Executive Director of New Hope Counseling Centers in metro New York. Dr. Ellison is the author/editor of six previous books, including *Healing for the City: Counseling for the Urban Setting*. He has had articles published in a wide variety of Christian periodicals including *Christianity Today* and *Leadership*.

Dr. Ellison hosts "Perspectives on Personal Living," a weekly broadcast heard nationwide. He is also a member of the National Advisory Board of the American Association of Christian Counselors and is a contributing editor for the *Journal of Psychology and Theology*.